DATE DUE

OCT 4 1990		
JUL 28 1992		

The Jock's Itch

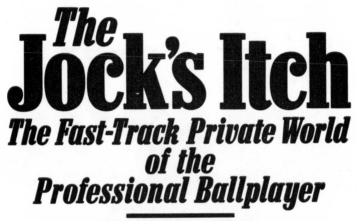

The Jock's Itch

The Fast-Track Private World of the Professional Ballplayer

TOM HOUSE, Ph.D.
Forewords by Matt Mitchell, Ph.D.,
and John Fuller, M.A.

**CONTEMPORARY
BOOKS**

CHICAGO · NEW YORK

Library of Congress Cataloging-in-Publication Data

House, Tom.
    The jock's itch : the fast-track private world of the
professional ballplayer / Tom House.
        p.   cm.
    ISBN 0-8092-4779-8
    1. Baseball players—Psychology.   I. Title.
GV867.3.H67   1989
796.357′019—dc19   89-520
                                                           CIP

Published by Contemporary Books, Inc.
180 North Michigan Avenue, Chicago, Illinois 60601
Manufactured in the United States of America
Library of Congress Catalog Card Number: 89-520
International Standard Book Number: 0-8092-4779-8

Published simultaneously in Canada by Beaverbooks, Ltd.
195 Allstate Parkway, Valleywood Business Park
Markham, Ontario L3R 4T8 Canada

To my real family: Karren, my wife, and Brittany, Brooke, and Bryan, my children. To my extended family: baseball. And to the fact that they both put up with each other for 22 years.

Contents

Foreword

My association with Tom House began on a road trip with the Richmond Braves in 1972, just after I'd joined the club. Tom was a crafty veteran Triple-A pitcher, a little lefty overachiever on the verge of a promising major league career. I was a left-handed outfielder trying to determine whether I was a prospect or a suspect. One night during my first week, I found myself talking with Tom in a hallway of the Commodore Perry Hotel after a game in which we'd both screwed up (misery loves company!). We discussed our lives, our wives, our goals and expectations until the wee hours of the morning. It was a significant moment for me since, up to that time, many of the players seemed to be, intellectually, somewhere between brain dead and one-dimensional. The conversation led to a friendship and business relationship that continues to thrive today.

Tom approaches writing the same way he approached pitching, the same way he lives his life: plan your work; work your plan; work to identify strengths and weaknesses; remember problems are only opportunities in disguise; be mentally tough; and try to have a big heart and a little empathy for everyone. *The Jock's Itch* does not aim to be sensational. The book is an accurate, chronological depiction of elite ballplayers' lives, from career beginnings to career endings. It provides insight into the developmental stages of young competitors as well as a look into the pitfalls of what Tom calls terminal adolescent syndrome—the jock's itch. He writes about himself, but the script is basically the same for most professional athletes.

A major reason Tom authored *The Jock's Itch* is that it was a chance to explore and explain the pro ballplayer's problems of reintegration into the real world after being released from sports. Actually, it's not a reintegration but an integration into reality, since most professionals have *never* been part of the "standard" civilian life. For reasons that will probably appear only in psychological publications, superior athletes are deemed special by parents, coaches, teachers, and peers at an early age. As a result of dysfunctional support received from others, athletic skills, narcissism, and conditional acceptance are the only portions of their being that get nourished. Every athlete must have some tunnel vision and concentrate only on his abilities to survive in the playing environment, but this tunnel vision becomes a handicap when the playing days end.

In all fairness to the athletes, it's not all their

fault. They have very little awareness of how or why their personalities evolved in a particular direction.

I consider myself to be one of the fortunate ex-professional baseball players. I quit after seven minor league seasons and a "cup of coffee" for half a season in the big leagues. In retrospect, I realize I did not want my ego crushed by the Braves' showing me the exit; I chose to find my own way out. Nevertheless, it wasn't until I had been in law enforcement more than fourteen years (still seeking those adrenaline highs), before graduate work in counseling psychology started to help me focus on the difficulties I've had with walking away from the game.

In conducting sports and family counseling, I have found, as Tom has found, that not all ballplayers feel a conscious psychological pain after their separation from the game. I for example, repressed my emotional attachment to the game from the day I quit. And, even with my work in psychology, I didn't realize it until the movie *Bull Durham* came out. I came apart in the parking lot following the movie—I'd actually played in the stadium featured in the film and really connected with some of the scenes. The experience was cathartic for me even after fourteen years away from the game.

I had a minor league manager who used to quip "It's not your life, it's not your wife" in an attempt to minimize the importance of the game of baseball relative to the real world. This was the closest thing to counseling I ever heard to prepare me for civilian living . It doesn't take a Rhodes scholar to calculate baseball's high attrition rate, and, despite all the negatives involved when a player's career is over, even a short career is usually an experience a player wouldn't trade for anything. My point is: Why should a pro ballplayer have a career followed by the pain and frustration of being integrated into the real world when he could have his career *without* the subsequent pain? By facing his problems while still in the game, by being aware of *who* he is rather than *what* he is, by keeping in mind that baseball means nothing to a billion Chinese, a player can better adjust to living a full and happy life after he's lost that special status of being a professional athlete.

Tom has researched the broader implications of organized baseball and its effect on the players' lives. *The Jock's Itch* is new information—entertaining and useful reading for players, parents, coaches, wives, and anyone interested in athletes as people.

John Fuller, M.A.
Sports Counselor

Foreword

An athlete is not born with the jock's itch. Terminal adolescent syndrome begins to form as soon as anyone, including the athlete himself, exhibits skills in a sport superior to those of his peers. The more apparent the skills—or the taller or heavier or faster or stronger the youngster is than those around him—the more likely he is to be put on a pedestal.

Once on a pedestal, the athlete begins to receive conditional treatment. The message is usually covert: "Make the team and you'll be popular"; "The more letters you win in high school, the bigger star you'll be"; "Don't worry about studying for the big test because we know you've got an important game. You can take tests the rest of your life." The messages come in a negative form as well, from mom or dad or coach: "Next time you make an error that costs your team a game, you won't get steak for dinner"; "Drop another pass, strike out with the bases loaded, miss a lay-up/a tackle/a kill at the net/a two-foot putt, and you're restricted to your room or you have to run extra laps/make twenty-five consecutive free throws/lift more weights/do a hundred push-ups/pedal that cycle an extra fifty miles. . . ."

In other words, we (family members, coaches, teachers) will accept you and love you only if you succeed. We'll love the rest of the children unconditionally, just because they are who they are. But you, young budding superstar, had better *always* live up to your potential, or you won't get our approbation, let alone our love. A lack of unconditional love is generally what starts an athlete off on the tortuous path of terminal adolescent syndrome.

The more the athlete perceives conditionality, the more he develops personality disorders of obsessive behavior, narcissism, and paranoia. Ironically, to be a successful world-class or professional athlete, these same quirks of personality seem to be as necessary as strength, speed, concentration, coordination, and a seemingly endless appetite for self-improvement and skill enhancement.

Without obsessive tendencies, the potential athlete probably won't have the capacity to spend the countless hours to develop the required skills to be the best at his sport. Without a good dose of narcissistic tendencies (athletes never meet mirrors they don't like), the athlete might not push, prod, pull, and pummel his body into the best shape possible for his sport. And an athlete without some strong paranoia is one who won't last very long at any level of sport. There's always fear of a younger, faster, stronger, better athlete coming along who is dead-set on taking his place, and the paranoid athlete may be able to prolong his career because looking over his shoulder at the ever-advancing competition will make him work harder.

Incidentally, I've been using "he" exclusively in this foreword not to be a male chauvinist but rather because female athletes haven't been studied and observed over the years in the same manner or as frequently as male athletes have. With the exceptions of professional tennis or golf, there aren't a lot of postcollegiate athletic careers for women—yet. Thus, there just haven't been enough opportunities to see if women in professional sports have the same, or similar, herd instincts as men—instincts so tellingly amplified in *The Jock's Itch.*

How can parents encourage their potential athletes without creating the possibility of future aberrant behavior?

Family order and discipline should not be sacrificed for the potential star athlete. Some sacrifices, such as getting a swimmer or skater to early-morning workouts or providing special expensive coaching, may be necessary, but that doesn't mean the youngster should be exempted from contributing to the family and doing the "normal" things he would have been doing if he weren't athletically inclined. Also, the family should insist that the athlete's teachers never allow him to slide by on his schoolwork or allow the athlete to make his studies secondary to his sport. Don't take the kid away from being a kid, and don't allow the kid to become a miniature professional athlete before his time.

A family's message should never be "Prove to us you have value. Be quite a bit better than the best you can be or hit the road and be a loser all your life." Instead the family should treat the future star with unconditional love. "It's too bad," Mom might say, "that you struck out with the bases loaded to end the game. Win or lose, we still love you. Whether you hit a home run or strike out, if you did your very best, that's all anyone can ever ask of you." If this seems a simple commonsense approach to preventing a young star from contracting the jock's itch, that's because it is.

But what about an aging athlete who is about to leave or has already left sports and been forced to enter the real world even as he clings to his glory days? What can his wife, family, and friends do to help switch off his terminal adolescent syndrome?

Dealing with the problem after the monster has been created is far more difficult than helping a youngster avoid it. However, it is vital to get the current or former athlete functioning at his highest capacity in the real world, a place he perhaps has never known well. While all of us, theoretically at least, continue to grow throughout our lives, the athlete has to grow *up* first so that he'll then be able to grow.

The athlete cannot do it on his own; he requires specific psychological work, a sort of emotional carpentry to reshape his self-concepts. To change, however, the aging athlete must first of all *want* to alter his perceptions of himself and of the world. He won't be able to continue to be the same old jock he's always been, nor will he be able to encourage others to keep him on that pedestal.

To deal with the entrenched mind-set of an athlete, it is helpful if his counselor/therapist has a competitive athletic background as well. The athlete's transition to the real world will be slower if he feels his therapist doesn't have a clue about what he has been through in his life and career. Progress can be fairly rapid, particularly if the therapist uses the jock's obsessive and narcissistic energies as positive tools rather than as negative factors.

The athlete should get the bulk of the psychological work and attention, but for his transition to be as complete and successful as possible, some family sessions are often required as well. This is because the athlete's changes lead to the realignment of everyone's roles. His wife finally gets to be *just* the wife and mother to their children rather than also an adjunct to some famous jock. She gets her own identity, and so do the children, who now get recognized for themselves rather than for Dad's feats. Sometimes, in order to incorporate and accomplish as many changes as possible, it may even be necessary to directly involve the athlete's parents in the therapy process.

Fortunately, there *is* help for terminal adolescence. Improvement takes hard work, perseverance, and dedication. The same qualities that helped create the mess in the first place can also be used to create a happy, well-adjusted adult with a fascinating past—but without a frustrating present and future.

Athletes, wives, family members, or friends who have questions or need help can contact us for assistance at (619) 536-9725 (The Center for Performance and Health, 9760 Caminito Doha, San Diego, CA 92131) or (714) 837-8130 (Biokinetics, 23547 Moulton Parkway, Suite 213, Laguna Hills, CA 92653).

Matt Mitchell, Ph.D.
Sports Psychologist

Acknowledgments

Thanks to my mom and dad; Rod DeDeaux, head coach at USC; Clyde King, my minor league manager in Atlanta; Ballard Smith, former president of the San Diego Padres; and the Texas Rangers baseball club.

The Jock's Itch

1
The Itch They Can't Scratch

You get paid to play a game, for God's sake. Thirty-three thousand dollars every two weeks as long as you keep putting up the numbers. TV, radio, newspapers, magazines, books, women, parties, and glory. Running with the guys, on the field and off. Personal appearances worth five grand a shot—just call my agent. And get me that car deal: I need that new Mercedes, and one for my mom, too. Look at me, world: I got nowhere to go but up, and I ain't looking back.

That's the profile: jet jocks with no fears or thoughts of tomorrow because they have no cares or worries, right?

Wrong. Read my lips, sports fans, there's another story. A real story about grown men who can hit a ball three hundred feet but can't balance a checkbook. Adult males who can memorize complex strategies and signals, but miss a bus because they can't remember to leave a wake-up call. Genetic supermen who can compete with fifty thousand screaming fans booing at them, but freeze up talking to twelve little kids at a Boy Scout dinner. Loving husbands and fathers who turn from Jekyll to Hyde in the blink of an eye, throwing sudden preadolescent temper tantrums or becoming hedonistic, narcissistic brats with the morals of a streetwalker. These are committed family men who are surrounded by supportive families—mothers, fathers, brothers, sisters, wives, children—but who spend two-thirds of their lives being influenced by the rules and rituals of their *sports* family: their teammates. And, when it's all over, they are nothing more than ex-athletes doomed to an existence of frustration and unhappiness because they don't have the skills to compete in the game of real life.

If you only see them between the white lines, these men who play games for a living, they have it all. Looks, health, money, fame—lots of each. Away from the ballpark, though, away from the cameras and crowds, what is their real story? What are they really like? How do they act? And how do they get away with those things that most people can only dream of?

This is a show-and-tell book. *Ball Four*-ish, yes, but introspective and self-helpish too, because sports is never going to change, only the people who play and watch. What we'll talk about here is serious, but maybe we'll have some fun talking about what happens and trying to explain *why* it happens. The wheel of big-time sports can't be rebuilt, but it sure can be greased up a little.

Have you ever had an itch you can't scratch? Athletes have one for life, a "jock's itch" that a ton of Tinactin won't cure. It's a malady that leads to infidelity, drug abuse, alcoholism, bankruptcy, and most of the other fashionable disasters you hear about today. My goal here isn't to tell you nasty stories about what's happening in the back of the bus—you can pick up a newspaper for that—but to open some of sports' discreetly sealed doors and talk about what happens to athletes *away* from the field, away from the lights and the crowds, away from where you can watch them.

The jock's itch: a condition that causes thirty-year-old men to act the same way they did when they were thirteen. A state of mind that simply refuses to absorb (or even consider) the reality that they'll be "over the hill" in their jobs before most men their age are even settled into a career. A burning itch to have it all, right now, before the quarter runs out and the ride is over—an itch that stays around long after the ride is over.

What makes me an expert? I have lived it, observed it, experienced it, researched it, succeeded in it, and failed in it. There is nothing in this book I haven't had personal experience with: I've been bankrupt; I've fallen into infidelity traps; I've abused substances; I've used and abused sports, and sports has used and abused me.

But through it all, I am still in sports after a twenty-two-year baseball career, as a player and as a coach (currently with the Texas Rangers). I am still married to the same woman. And I still love both. Unfortunately, many of my peers have been less fortunate. In fact, after watching so many of them suffer through failed marriages, drug and alcohol rehabilitation, financial ruin, and many other disasters, I decided to go back to school for a doctorate in psychology, to research and write a thesis on terminal adolescence and to find some answers. I hope that what I found will be as full of insight for you as it was for me.

He *is* different. He can get away with things that you can only imagine, and he can do it because at some point in his charmed life, someone convinced him he was special. Oh, he's known it for a long time, since he was a kid, from the day the teacher excused him from doing his homework because of the big game or his family postponed dinner again until he got home from practice. He always knew he'd get the best girl, the most friends, decent grades, and all the back-patting one guy can handle in a lifetime. And when he makes it big in sports, especially professional sports, he's completely confident that no one can ever take this all away from him. He was special then, he is special now, and he will be special forever and ever.

Whew! Sounds like quite a life, doesn't it? Nothing but rewards and people who can't do enough for you? Well, for the elite athlete, it has always been this way, from the time he was a youngster. It doesn't take him long to get used to people bending over backward to accommodate him, helping him, changing their plans to fit his. Before he's out of grade school, everyone knows him as the stud. His family attends every game, the girls all scream for him, the guys wish they could play as well. His coach sees pennants, his teachers see Ds but are willing to give Cs since he's playing so hard. At thirteen, he's a bona fide star.

By the time he's in high school, he's having dreams of going professional, and in the local paper, a reporter writes that there's a good chance this could happen. Someone claims to have seen a scout in the stands at the last game, maybe from the Yankees. The kid's mother runs out of room in the scrapbook, and starts another. His father puts the trophies in the front hall, where everyone can see them. He's never been so proud.

Eventually word gets around that this kid is a real sensation, and sure enough, some scouts and college coaches come calling. The kid's going places. From his perspective, this doesn't really come as much of a surprise. After all, he's gifted; he's better than any other player in town, maybe in the state. And now his dream is coming true.

Now let's skip ahead a few years. He's a big-league veteran, making the big money and living the good life. He's realized his dreams of playing professional ball, being famous, signing autographs and going to great parties and being on television and getting paid to wear certain shoes. And he's been especially lucky because he's playing so well that he can get away with things that other players can't, like the time he got caught smoking that joint in the back of the bus or when he missed practice because he was so hung over from the night before, and besides he just couldn't get that girl out of his room. He knows that other players would have been nailed—to the wall—but since he was doing his job with such success, well, they let it go. It does occur to him that his talents have afforded him some very special treatment, but it never, *ever* occurs to him that the special treatment will disappear as soon as his talents begin to wane. He lives by the belief that he is charmed; he doesn't realize that one day the charm is going to tarnish and turn green all over him.

This is the psychological makeup of the professional ballplayer, a child in a man's body, an adult who defines the expression that "baseball is a little boys' game being played by grown men." The adult ballplayer is only a little more mature, advanced, or emotionally wise than he was when he was a kid playing Little League or high-school ball.

He is for all practical purposes terminally adolescent.

Put simply, he's never really grown up, because he's never had to. His sense of responsibility has always begun and ended with competition at the stadium. From the time he was a kid, other people were willing to pick up after him, make excuses for him, support him in every way. As he grew older, those support systems just became more sophisticated. The women became more beautiful, the fans more adoring, and instead of getting pats on the back he began receiving lots of money.

So, you might ask, what's wrong with that? If the guy's lucky enough to be so genetically superior that he can play a sport at a skill level that only a few hundred people can match, why shouldn't he reap the benefits? The answer is simple: he is *still* of the same mind-set when he is no longer a professional athlete! At that point, he becomes a "civilian" with few abilities, talents, or skills that he can apply to the nonbaseball world. He's also without the real world experience and maturity to figure out how to cope.

If you are a brilliant mathematician, or a brilliant musician or doctor, you, too, may receive special treatment your entire life. But you can do your math or your music or your medicine for a lifetime. An athlete has to stop when his body tells him to. Suddenly he's launched from his sports-world mentality actually old and washed up before middle age.

And here's where the "jock's itch" becomes a force: a professional ballplayer cannot imagine, ever, that his career might one day come to an end. It's called positive denial. Oh, he may know it deep down in his heart, but in his head, he is bound to the concept that he is one of the "chosen." And therefore, nothing will ever come between him and his sport, and no one will ever chastise him for behavior that is unacceptable in the real world. Special people get special favors.

So if he does too many drugs, or he gets caught cheating on his wife, or if he makes a few bad investments, he's positive that someone will be there to bail him out. After all, that's the way it's always been, right?

But let's be real—it *will* eventually end and it *won't* always be that way. Consider: average length of major league career: four years plus sixty days, major and minor leagues combined. That's not a whole lot of time to learn the ropes, become a starter, become a superstar, then a megastar, then count all your money and buy your own time. That's barely enough time to get your name in *The Baseball Encyclopedia*.

Ah, but while you are hanging on to your baseball career for dear life, you'll have nothing *but* time for the game—you kiss everything else goodbye, and you do it gladly. Length of scheduled season: 240 days, spring training and regular season combined. Road trips away from family: 81 to 120 days. Time for off-season commitments: between 60 and 110 days per year. In short, all the baseball one man can handle.

With that, of course, comes the visibility profile. National and local newspaper exposure related to the sport: 200 days per year, days that the guy can actually pick up a paper and see his name in print in some way, shape, or form. Other magazines: 30 days per year. Local radio exposure relating to the sport: 200 days per year. Local and regional television exposure related to the sport: 62 days per year. National television exposure related to the sport: 10 days per year.

It is a fishbowl, a spotlight no one could escape, and few even try. Keeping a perspective on reality would be difficult for any developmentally *normal* individual. The athlete, the terminal adolescent, hasn't got a chance.

Throughout this book, as we take a close look at the *real* life existence of the ballplayers you see on the field, you'll see how terminal adolescence affects practically every athlete in the game, and why it's so difficult for players to live a normal, mature lifestyle. When one signs a professional contract, some time during that signing a critical line is crossed. To some degree, from this point on, the terminal adolescence syndrome, the jock's itch, will affect every player's life. No matter how successful or unsuccessful he might become in other portions of his life, the jock's itch will always be an integral part of his makeup.

Turning professional means taking a virtually irreversible step toward long-term mental and emotional adolescence. Unfortunately, the longer the professional career, the longer the exposure to the professional baseball environment and the further athletes will drift from an ability to understand and cope with the demands of the real world. Professional baseball becomes an arena where the world is ruled by competition, ritual, tradition, and lifestyle. Professional players will never again be completely satisfied with nonsports living and working. Maybe someday they'll appear *outwardly* successful, but they will never be able to inwardly achieve the type of feedback they once derived from baseball.

In a world where agents, public relations directors, traveling secretaries, clubhouse attendants, wives, and friends have always made most off-the-field decisions and done work that normally would help create and sustain a complete personality profile, athletes are out of luck. Once used to traveling for two-thirds of the year, athletes in retirement experience boredom and the old "thrill-me" factor. Gone are the bright lights and celebrity status, the mental and physical joyrides, the temptations of a life away from home with no consequences, and the exhilarating bonus that comes with the territory of being a high-profile competitive athlete.

This book is for everyone who has ever watched a ballplayer and sighed, "What I would give to be in his shoes." I guarantee that by the time you've finished reading, you'll feel different.

2
Run Silent, Run Deep
Baseball's Unwritten Rules

If life were the movies, the most successful ballplayers would be the nicest guys, and the minor leagues would be filled with all the socially outcast bad guys. Your ERA would be based on how many times a week you went to church, and you'd get a hit for every good deed you did. Anyone who dared argue with his manager would automatically be sent down to Double-A, and anyone caught using drugs would be drummed out of baseball forever. In other words, players would be judged by their personalities, not their performance.

But welcome to the real baseball world, where it really doesn't matter *what* you are as a person, only what you are as a player. Can you hit home runs? Fine, we'll overlook that drunk-driving charge. Just don't ruffle any feathers, and we'll all just get along fine, as long as you keep up the good work.

11

In baseball, the name of the game is fitting in. You can be a real jerk, but if you play by the invisible rules and adhere to the rituals and traditions that have been in place since baseball began more than a hundred years ago, then you'll be just fine. And you'd better not take too long to figure out exactly what those rules are—if you can't be programmed within the first year, so long, kid.

When I first became a professional ballplayer, in 1967, I was a slightly cocky left-handed pitcher from the University of Southern California, with one of the best collegiate programs in the country, under the direction of the great Rod Dedeaux. I was going to tear up the big leagues. Weren't we all? . . .

I signed with the Braves organization and flew off to Atlanta to meet the bigwigs. It was magnificent. I got to throw batting practice to the big-league ball club, was wined and dined. Hey, welcome to the organization. It was really a great day.

The next morning I got on a plane bound for the minor leagues—Kinston, North Carolina, where their Class A team is. Now, remember, I've just come from a USC Trojan collegiate program where we had two sets of whites, two sets of grays, free gloves and shoes, first-class hotels and air travel. Strictly first class.

I arrive in the pouring rain in Kinston, wearing my navy blue blazer, blue slacks, and striped tie— Mr. Preppy ready for action.

Talk about rude awakenings, penthouse to outhouse. The general manager for the Kinston Eagles picks me up at the airport and says, "Just throw your bags and yourself in the back of the pickup truck. Jump on in and pull that tarp over your head."

I'm thinking, "Wow, okay, I guess I can put up with this," except for the fact that his fucking dog is riding up front in the cab. No big deal. I suck it up, arrive at the ballpark a little damp, get my introduction, walk around, "Hi, how are you doing?" They give me a locker on the far end of the clubhouse, which boils down to a little partition with about six nails.

Right away the skipper, Andy Pafko, calls a team meeting. He stands up in his inimitable way and says, "I want all the California ballplayers on that side of the clubhouse. Everybody else come over here with me." And he proceeds to tell everyone else to "stay the fuck away" from California ballplayers because they're weird and a detriment to baseball. California is the fucking land of fruits and nuts, he says.

Here I am, brand new to the ball club, raising the eyebrows and wondering, Jesus Christ tomatoes, what have I got myself into?

Still, I am excited to be a Brave, a member of the Braves organization, and I decide I'm just going to make the best of this no matter what. So after the meeting I slide on over to the equipment manager and clubhouse boy/God, and I get my uniform. It turns out to be one of those woollies with the tomahawk from the Braves' Milwaukee days.

I end up with Joe Adcock's old top and pants, size forty-four, and I can fit my whole body in one of the legs. Needless to say, my cool, breezy attitude about being a professional athlete is taking a severe beating.

Pafko (who, it turns out, is a great guy) walks by and says, "I'll talk to you after B.P." "Sure thing, coach," I say, to which he responds, "Call me coach again and I'll fine you $25—I'm your manager or Skipper. Got it?" "Sure thing, Skipper."

Later we sit on the bench, game about ready to start, and I'm told, "Well, we're not going to start you right away. We are going to maybe work you in a couple innings of relief, and then we'll give you a start later in the week."

So I'm riding the pine watching the world go by, watching infield practice, and I notice that our starting pitcher, John Stewart (a California ballplayer, by the way), is warming up to go in the game, and he's not wearing socks. Stirrups, but no socks. And I'm going, "Hmmm, what's going on here," so I very quietly slide up to one of my teammates and say, "Hey, what's the scoop with John? How come he's not wearing any socks?" And the guy says, "Well, the owner wants us to buy our own sanitary socks, and John figures it's not something we should do, so he is just going to pitch without 'em."

Now the blush is wearing quite thin on my first day of professional baseball. Reality is beginning to set in. I look out over the ballpark and see a real old field, ill kept. I see decaying stands. I see only a handful of fans sitting in the stands. I see lights that have the candlepower of a twenty-five-watt bulb. It's musty, rainy, mosquitoey, sweaty, and I'm sitting in a too-big wool uniform, already having been identified as a "California ballplayer." Strange existence.

And so begins the indoctrination, the defining of the traditions, rules, rituals, ethics, and roles that a hundred years of professional baseball dictate a young athlete must survive and adapt to if he wants to exist in the game.

My next day at the park begins abruptly when one of the veteran ballplayers, a guy named Hal Breeden who had been in A ball for three or four years by that time, says, "Let's go play some pepper, Rook," and I say, "Sure, let's go play some pepper." This is about an hour before batting practice is supposed to start.

I notice everyone's looking at us funny, but I just figure it's part of the program. I am a little naive—well not a *little* naive, but a *lot* naive, actually—and we start playing pepper.

Well, Breeden just annihilates everything I throw. He is not playing pepper. He is taking batting practice, except that I'm standing twenty-five to thirty feet away. These bullets are blowing by me, and I don't really want to scream because I'm new and I'm trying to be macho and show I belong, but I'm thinking that this is a pretty dangerous game to play just so this jerk can see what I'm made of.

So, after the fifteenth or sixteenth throw, he hits a burner off my leg. I say, "Hey, Hal, this is not fun. Why don't you find some other idiot to be your gopher with this pepper stuff?" And I walk away.

And he says, "Fuck you, rookie. Who the fuck do you think you are? Just because you're a number-three draft choice doesn't make you a prospect. You're a suspect, just like us. Kiss my ass."

And right away it's crystal clear: the pressures involved with being a "prospect" and the pressures involved with being a survivor, like Hal, are different. And many times, especially in the minor leagues—especially in the *lower* minor leagues, they're almost a deterrent to a team getting along. But it's my job to fit in, and these veterans were being damn sure I did.

Off-the-field living accommodations? Forget it. Most everybody on the ballclub stayed in an apartment complex called Vanity Arms, affectionately dubbed Insanity Arms by the people who stayed there. I ended up bunking with four other guys in a two-bedroom apartment. I had one corner of a couch for a hundred bucks a month. Eat your own food as you purchased it and survive everywhere else you can.

Meal money on the road was $3.50 a day. Now you know where the expression "bush leagues" comes from. The most you could make as a new signee was five hundred dollars a month.

Anyway, the summer progressed, with its twenty-three-hour bus rides, and I played the role of a typical first-year player trying to make the adjustments to a professional baseball environment.

As luck would have it, the Braves called me up to pitch for their Triple-A ball club against the major league ball club in an exhibition game in Richmond, Virginia. I went seven-plus innings; did a real good job. Even got a couple of base hits. Must have proved something to somebody, because they told me to join the Richmond club as soon as I could move my stuff to Virginia.

So I finished the summer in Richmond—and spent the next four and a half summers in Richmond, Virginia, Triple-A ball, pushing up daisies trying to figure out what the hell I had to do to get going. I was stuck in what would become a five-year minor league career, which is best described by saying that those first lousy months in Kinston were the best.

The next year I got invited to major league camp. I left my wife behind with her mom and dad and all our possessions, and I headed for spring training fully convinced that I was going to make the big-league ball club.

I got picked up at the airport, and, as it turned out, a couple of major leaguers had flown in the same time I did, so we all piled in together. We were driven to the Ramada Inn on the Green right across from the ballpark, West Palm Beach Municipal Stadium, which is quite nice. I start to get out, but the driver/clubhouse kid says, "You're going down to the magnificent Alma Hotel," which was where the minor league players or invitees to major league camp stayed.

What a place. The first four floors were a retirement home for the elderly. The rest of the seven floors were where the athletes stayed. The best assessment of the Alma Hotel was that they would have to paint the place to condemn it.

My roommates were Ron Schueler and Bobby Didier, two big-leaguers-to-be, great guys. Ron was a beer drinker. Bobby was a nineteen-year-old whose father was a scout in the organization.

It was a nightmare. Breakfast in the morning

was scary, lunch was soup at the ballpark, and dinner was basically whatever they served at the Alma Hotel. We tried to avoid it as much as possible. We were surrounded by senile people and screaming ambulances. A real ballplayer's existence.

In light of today's approach to minor league athletes, which is considerably more humane, it is unbelievable what they used to put kids through in order to initiate them into professional baseball.

But you adjust. Out of desperation and a sense of survival, you learn fast, and you accept what is being dished out because it's the only way.

I ended up with the Double-A ballclub at the end of spring training, with the promise that I'd be sent up to Triple-A ten days later, when the season started. True to baseball tradition—and it's still true today—baseball will tell an athlete whatever he wants to hear in order to get him to do what he is supposed to.

So I went to Double-A in Shreveport with the understanding that I'd head to Triple-A, Richmond, in a few days. In other words, I was a Triple-A ballplayer who was getting a head start by pitching a couple of ball games in Double-A.

Well, a month into the season I was still in Shreveport wondering when I'm going to get called up. I finally said, "Well, I guess maybe this may or may not happen, so I'm going to get my wife down here and get a place and just scuffle any way I can." Karren showed up on a Friday, spent the weekend finding and renting an apartment, and as we're getting ready to go on a Monday road trip, the phone call comes: "You're going to Richmond." So long, Shreveport. So long, apartment deposit.

Here we come, Richmond Braves and Triple-A baseball, wahoo! In Triple-A, you fly some of the time, bus some of the time. Meal money was ten bucks a day, heavy-duty stuff. The big leagues are just a heartbeat and a five game win streak away.

The Richmond team, at this point in time, consisted of some pretty grizzled veterans, athletes on the way out and/or career Triple-A ballplayers. It was hard-core. These guys had been in the wars.

I couldn't get over how many people smoked and how many people drank and how many people smoked and drank and kept late hours and got themselves going the next day with these magic little triangular pills, things they called greenies.

It was a real tough year for both Karren and me. We were square pegs in round holes, young at twenty-one and twenty, the youngest couple on the club. Almost all of the wives had been in the game for a while; there were lots of children. Many of the ballpark women were, well, I wouldn't say hardcore, but they were runners. They had seen their share.

The ballplayers themselves, while I found them entertaining, really didn't let me fit in. I was just a goofy left-hander from California who was a little hyper and did things a little more strangely than most and overreacted when I shouldn't overreact. I was making my rookie mistakes in a veteran environment and suffering the consequences.

Karren, from a personal standpoint, was really devastated; she didn't really interact. People were nice to her, but she was very, very lonely playing at playing house, playing at being married. So, in order to get through the summer, without telling me she just stopped taking birth-control pills and got pregnant.

I remember finding out. I was in Niagara Falls, and we had just played the Buffalo ball club. I pitched that night and got my drawers blown off, and I'm considering committing suicide, looking out the sixth-floor window of the Niagara Hotel, when the phone rings, and Karren says, "Hey, guess what? We're pregnant."

Oh boy, I thought, feeling my rear end pucker. Let's put some more pressure on me. What am I doing here? When am I going to get someone out?

Talk about feeling overmatched. I can remember throwing what I thought was my best curveball, my best collegiate curveball that nobody ever hit hard at USC, to a young catcher from Louisville, and he hit it about four hundred fifty feet, and as he's running around the bases I'm saying to myself, "Jesus Christ tomatoes, I'm in a league I don't belong in. Dear Mom, I'll be home soon—they're hitting everything I'm throwing up here."

Well, I also began to realize that skill levels and talent levels and experience levels all make a difference. The guy who hit the home run off me was a young fellow named Johnny Bench. I began to see that as you get closer and closer to the top of the pyramid, big-league baseball, it gets tougher and tougher to survive.

That was the season I finally learned about what it took to survive in a professional baseball environment. I was the guy who didn't really fit in, and if I didn't realize it then, I can sure tell you now: you've got to fill a role on the team if you're going to make it in the game. That's how the system survives. Back then, I really didn't know who I was, baseballwise; I think if there was any impression of me from the outside looking at me, it would be that I was just a little goofy, and probably because I was left-handed. I hid behind that for a while.

I was a hard worker, and I think my hard work and dedication helped others be patient with my overemotional, naive approach to the game. One salty old catcher said, after watching me get excited about a couple of calls, that if he ever wanted to really get up for a ball game, he was going to get a big glass of water and take me instead of a greenie.

So I didn't fall into any of the categories that normal ballplayers would find and identify themselves with. I wasn't a hunter or a fisherman. I didn't drink or take drugs. I had just gotten married, and I wasn't hardly religious.

But at this point in time, all of that was a negative in the eyes of many people, as if it detracted from my ability to perform in a professional baseball environment.

And here's the point to this little saga: when you're in the professional baseball environment, as I had been at this point for a year and a half, there is a whole helluva lot of social and emotional programming going on. They're getting you ready for the bigs, kid. In the clubhouse, on the field and off the field.

It's overt, it's covert. There are rules and ethics and roles and a whole lot of little things that there's just no way you can possibly explain. And it's not something that anyone *has* explained. There are no written rules passed down from whenever—a hundred years of game transition and people transitions and traveling and sweating and jockstraps and cuts and trains and planes and buses and succeeding and failing make the rules, and you have to figure them out. You learn what's acceptable and not acceptable and where you fit and where you don't fit, and the only way you learn is by basically fucking up. It is a dance, a balance, a system of human interaction.

In essence, you've become part of an extended family, made up of a number of individuals of varying talents and psychoemotional makeups, from a number of different backgrounds and a number of different demographic areas, but the common denominator is that you now have a family, an entity, a system that is unique to yourself and the people you're in the system with. For some it's really the only family they will ever know and understand. And just as you'd protect and shelter your real family, you shelter your baseball family.

The best way to explain it is to recall the pioneers coming across the country. Wherever they were in their wagon trains, when it came time to settle in, they'd circle the wagons. No matter what the environmental change was, when the wagons got where they were going to go, they circled the wagons and carried on inside the circle of wagons just as they had in St. Louis or Chattanooga, only now they're out in New Mexico. Everyone has a job to do, a role to fulfill.

It's the same with ballplayers, and it's amazing to watch a professional ball club roll into a clubhouse or roll into a spring-training environment or roll into an exhibition game. It's a dance, a performance. It's a stage setting where everybody has a part; everybody plays his part; who gets which locker, who sets up in what particular area of the clubhouse, what kind of music is played. It can occur in a terrible clubhouse in Fort Myers in a spring-training environment; it can occur in a hot, sweaty clubhouse in Columbus, Georgia. It can occur in one of the best clubhouses in the big leagues, at Arlington Stadium or Yankee Stadium. Wherever this group of athletes goes, it rolls, it happens, it works.

Baseball people know the second a stranger, a nonbaseball person—a "green fly," so to speak— walks into a clubhouse. It just affects the flow, the feel, the communication processes, the eye contact. When there is a nonbaseball person around the clubhouse or on the bench, it's very much the same as having a stranger walk into your kitchen and stand there while you're preparing a meal and the family is getting ready for dinner.

Just as a family has rites and routines, so does a ball club. For example, the rituals of bus ethics. Bus ethics? Yes, it may sound silly to you, but if it does, it's because you're not in baseball. In the baseball family, this is serious business. It doesn't matter if you're in a rookie league or the big leagues: whenever a team gets on the bus, certain ethics are recognized and have to be adhered to.

The manager sits in the front seat on the right of the bus. The only exception to this I ever witnessed was Frank Howard. When he was a manager or a coach, there was no way that he, being as large as he is, could fit in *any* seat. He stood on the bottom step near the door. But aside from him, managers sit in that front right seat.

Coaches will surround the manager, either right behind the driver or behind the manager. The manager usually has his seat all to himself. The only time someone will ever sit with him is when he calls a coach up to chat or if by chance the general manager happens to be riding along with him. Then the GM and the manager will sit together in that seat.

Beer drinkers are always in the back of the bus. You say to yourself, they're probably back there hiding because they're drinking beer. But beer is an acceptable part of baseball, and there is only one basic reason that beer drinkers sit in the back of the bus: it's closest to the bathroom.

Card players sit in the middle of the bus because on some of the bigger Greyhound and Trailways buses, those seats face each other with tables that come down from the top, so you can play cards there. Even when a bus doesn't have the tables, most of the card players will be right in the middle of the bus anyway, with a box in the aisle that they use for a card table.

Today's headphones and Walkman technology have, thank God, basically replaced ghetto blasters and the traveling stereos that made a lot of noise, but when boom boxes were the rage, the music guys would get as far away from the skipper as they possibly could, fighting each other to see whose music would be loud enough to drown out all the others (Springsteen vs. Michael Jackson, Willie Nelson vs. Van Halen), and fighting the beer drinkers for position in the back of the bus.

One of the strangest transitions for me, going from player to coach, was how uncomfortable I felt riding in the front of the bus. I had always been a back-of-the-bus guy because I was always in one of the back-of-the-bus groups, or else I was in the doghouse and needed to get as far away from the manager as possible. But it's amazing to watch these patterns, these ethics that are learned in the minor leagues and carried over into the big leagues, even on a real short ride from the airport to the ballpark, a twenty-minute or half-hour ride. Without fail, guys get on the bus and go right to the area they sat in when they rode the buses in the minor leagues. It's automatic.

*　　　　*　　　　*　　　　*

The baseball world is almost World-War-Two-ish in its reinforcement of protecting itself, something along the lines of "Loose lips sink ships." The message is: what you see here, what you say here, what you do here, *stays here.* That mentality is strictly observed, and any failure to do so is simply unacceptable. You toss out any other ethics or standards you learned in the "real" world, and you live by the rules that baseball dictates. You live your life in essentially two different worlds, with the understanding that what goes on in the baseball environment really has nothing to do with your feelings and emotions and commitments in the real world. The rules you must play by, the actions that are required to survive, are mutually exclusive, at least in a baseball player's mind. Only when the two worlds collide, when a guy gets caught cheating on his wife or tests positive for drugs or does something in the real world that can't be protected by the baseball world, does it become apparent that there is no way to mesh the two. In the real world, you have to pay. The problem is, a ballplayer spends so much time and energy on his baseball family that it becomes a real struggle to live up to the expectations his real-world family has for him.

The difference between the two lifestyles is amazing, and the conflicting expectations can be overwhelming. In the real world, a ballplayer has his role and his status as a father, a husband, a provider, the son of a guy who is now famous on the block. He truly does love his family, and he wouldn't do anything to hurt them; his goal is to make them proud.

But that's the Dr. Jekyll. The Mr. Hyde surfaces in the little protected baseball world that takes care of its own, in that fraternity of traditions and rituals that are as old as the game itself. And in that private baseball life, each player has a different set of roles to play and statuses to maintain.

On every baseball team, you have the drinkers, the druggies, the chasers, the sportsmen, the Bible toters, and the floaters. All athletes will fall into at least one of those categories—very seldom the same one forever, but always one of them or a combination of them. If this sounds like a gross generalization, it's only because in the real world it would be unthinkable for *everyone* to fit into one of these groups. But in the baseball world, if you don't fit into one of these, you don't fit in, period.

The appeal of these categories has changed over the years. Twenty or thirty years ago, the group to belong to was the drinkers. It represented the most socially and occupationally acceptable pastime. After ball games you hung around the clubhouse, drank beer, and told stories. It wasn't illegal, you could do it in public, and if you drank too much and fell down a lot it was entertaining as hell. Hey, Babe Ruth made a career of it. The only time anyone ever mentioned an "alcohol problem" was when the bartender ran out of ice.

In the seventies, drugs became more fashionable, and the druggies became an acceptable group, an expansion that certainly paralleled what society was going through at the time. Initially, drug use consisted of taking "greenies," or amphetamines. The philosophy was, You never got beat, you only got outgreened. When a guy hit a home run off you, you wanted to know what the hell he was on. But eventually the *real* drug culture began to emerge, and greenies became the least of baseball's drug concerns. We'll discuss this further in a later chapter.

Then you have the chasers, the guys who chase women to kill time. There is an adage that says, If you chase women, you better not drink or do drugs. If you're a serious drinker or a druggie, you don't specialize in chasing women. Too many poisons. If you are into any of these particular things, the late hours can shorten your career, and any combination of two (or more) of the three will definitely shorten it. You have to pick your poison and deal with it accordingly.

The sportsmen are essentially the hunters and fishermen and golfers. Most of these guys are drinkers, but they drink less than the real drinkers, and they chase, but they chase less than the real chasers. They like to hunt, they like to fish, they like to golf, and they like to talk about hunting, fishing, and golfing.

The Bible toters are growing in number; being religious has become much more acceptable. It used to be that the religious players who adhered to the "God's will" philosophy (whether you won or lost, it was God's will) were completely ostracized by baseball. Off the field these players were respected for their convictions, but on the field no one wanted the ball to be hit by a Bible toter when the game was on the line, and no one wanted that kind of player going to the plate when you had to have a base hit. Today that's all changed. Now you have players who use their beliefs to make them tougher: the feeling is, "I can do anything because God is on my side," as opposed to, "Whatever I do, even if I fail, it's God's will." There's considerably less of a stigma attached to Christianity in baseball than there once was.

When you don't fit into any of those categories, you're a turd—a floater. Floaters are, by process of elimination, individuals who aren't drinkers, druggies, chasers, sportsmen, or Bible toters. You can be a fitness freak. You can be a financial whiz. You can be a graduate student. You can be a nutritionist. But you're probably not going to fit; your teammates want to see you in one of those other categories, and individuality is not smiled upon. This is particularly true where young players are concerned; a rookie will be run out of town if he can't conform to the behavior his teammates have programmed him for.

I have been a floater most of my career. I have been in and out of the acceptable categories, some more than others, but overall I was a floater. It used to piss a lot of people off that I carried books in my briefcase instead of *Playboy*s and booze. As a floater, you have to make some serious choices: you can stick to your guns and remain a nonperson among your teammates, or you can force yourself to fit in and become a nonperson to yourself. Quite a choice. But look on the bright side—you have all these great groups to choose from! C'mon, what'll it be? Druggies, boozers, womanizers . . . join the party!

This division of personalities even extends to the demographics of the clubhouse, where players automatically cluster within their own group, around the type of people that they enjoy the most, the ones who listen to their kind of music, the ones who speak Spanish, the blacks, the white liberals, and the white rednecks. They will seek their own level.

Similarly, when players have to room together on the road, they will usually both belong to the same group. It's only logical that if you're going to room with a guy, you don't want him to be an early riser if you're a late-night partier, and conversely, you don't want him to be a chaser if you're a Bible toter.

Baseball rules also dictate that everyday players, the regulars, shouldn't room with pitchers. The reason for this isn't hard to figure: when a pitcher has a ball hit to the shortstop who happens to be his roommate, and roomie blows it and it costs the pitcher the game, it's going to be pretty intense back in the room that night.

Along those lines, there are many starting pitchers who do not like to room with relief pitchers, also for obvious reasons. When the short man comes in in the ninth inning and blows the starter's game, it's a little tough for them to share a bathroom later that night.

But all of this becomes a function of "the dance of the systems," that extended-family system that provides ballplayers with this home away from home. Usually, when you read about an athlete who has an "attitude problem" or "has trouble getting along," it's because he doesn't fit in, or is not willing to be slotted into one of the categories. In other words, he's not learning, accepting, and dealing with the rules and rituals and traditions of the insider's world of baseball. And unless such an athlete has superior talent and is indispensable to the team, he will wash out of the system within the first two or three years he's in professional baseball. Unless you can come to the party and get on the dance floor, you're not going to make it.

In my opinion, it takes a good three to five years to figure out how to cope and survive without ruffling people's feathers. It takes that long to come to terms with your baseball identity, to understand both the written rules and the unspoken rules. The written rules are managerial. The unwritten rules have twenty-five different interpretations, one for each man on the roster, based on how good you are, how good you could be, would be, should be, or how you're going to be dealt with when you screw up or cross a line that you shouldn't have crossed.

Put more simply, performance affects perception. Play great, and they'll overlook the fact that you're a jerk. Play lousy, and you'll pay. Peer-group pressure forces you to conform both in the clubhouse and on the field, and the ways and means range from subtle to blatant. If you screw up, someone's going to get the message to you.

Supposedly, that's what the fine system is for. Get 'em where it counts, right in the wallet. Sure. Managers can fine players, and players can fine themselves through kangaroo courts, but the real messages are being delivered with words and/or physical intimidation, which is probably a lot more devastating to an athlete than dollar fines. Every ball club has an "enforcer"—the guy who is responsible for getting your attention when you're in trouble. He's the one who lets you know that your drug dealer friends aren't welcome in the clubhouse, or that if you're going to stay out partying until sunrise, at least manage to get to the ballpark in time for batting practice. When your problem has escalated to the point where the enforcer has to take you out behind the center-field fence to get your attention, you have pretty much screwed up.

Fines in baseball have always been a joke to me, levied by the league, the organization, or by the kangaroo court. You never hear about fines when a team is winning; it's only when things are going tough that the answer is "discipline."

I remember flying into Montreal on an off-day, Thursday, for a Friday-Saturday-Sunday series with the Expos. Montreal can be a very exciting city, and the whole ball club went out on Thursday night to party. Unfortunately, our manager checked our rooms after curfew and nailed nineteen out of twenty-five ballplayers.

Well, there was a big team meeting on Friday before the ball game, and Skip says, "Okay, you assholes, I checked last night and nineteen out of the twenty-five guys were out. Tonight I'm checking again, and if I catch anybody out past curfew, it's going to be double the fine. The first fine was a hundred bucks, the second will be two hundred, so you assholes are looking at two hundred bucks when I check tonight."

So, of course, he checked that night, and this time there were twenty-three of twenty-five guys out past curfew.

You can see where this is going. Before the game on Saturday we have another team meeting. He is livid, just totally livid. He screams, "Okay, you stupid assholes, you sons of bitches, you nonproductive idiots, read my lips when I tell you this. I am checking tonight, and if any one of you assholes is *in* your room, is even *close* to your room, I am fining you five hundred bucks."

Then he adds, "You Jesus freaks better check into another fucking hotel, because I don't want any of you here either. You don't want to follow my rules. I'll change them for you. Let's do it the wrong way and we'll see how you do." There weren't very many heads that hit a pillow that night.

It was funny—it was also sad—but it was funny because we lost the two ball games after the nights when we were supposed to be in for curfew, and on Sunday, after we *had* to stay out all night, we just kicked Montreal's ass completely. I'm not sure what it proved, but it did show me that the manager can make rules and fine all he wants; the bottom line is that performance makes right—performance *on the field.*

It also proved that in the baseball world, you conform or you fail. I don't know what pissed off the manager more, that most of the team was out past curfew, or that the "Jesus freaks" wouldn't go along for the ride. Either way, the unwritten rule of the moment dictated that everyone go down together; those "good guys" who preferred to stay in had to get with the program and conform, like it or not.

Logical? Perhaps not. But realistic? Absolutely. We got rules, and you'll follow 'em, kid. Welcome to baseball's way.

3
The Game
Within the Game

It was every married athlete's road-trip nightmare. This future Hall-of-Famer was celebrating his birthday, and for the occasion he had "imported" a woman he had been involved with for a few months; suffice it to say she was not his wife. She arrived in town on Friday night while he was at the stadium and went straight to the hotel, letting herself into his room with the key he had left her at the front desk. She unpacked her bag, ordered a bottle of wine from room service, and settled into a big bubble bath to wait for Mr. Ballplayer.

Meanwhile, who is about to check into the same hotel but Mrs. Ballplayer, who has decided to surprise her husband on his birthday (although to call it a surprise would be something of an understatement in this case). She gets a key to his room, heads upstairs, opens the door, and, finding a strange woman in the tub, turns eleven shades of red because she thinks she walked into the wrong room.

"Oh, God," she stammers, "I thought this was So-and-so's room. I'm so sorry . . ." And she begins to leave.

But the woman in the tub, completely baffled as to why this woman was looking for Mr. Ballplayer, says, "This *is* his room, and who the fuck are you?"

At which point the wife turns five *more* shades of red and bellows to the entire hotel, "I'm the S.O.B.'s wife—who the fuck are *you*???!" And now that everyone is properly introduced, the "import" decides she'd better forget about the wine and find shelter elsewhere for the night.

About an hour later, Mr. Ballplayer finally gets back to the hotel and, in his blissful ignorance, throws open the door to his room expecting to find a very private birthday celebration.

Surprise.

We can all imagine, I'm sure, the scene that followed—crying, screaming, yelling, an occasional ashtray whipped across the room, and an eventual call to the lawyer or a six-hour therapy apology. Was he wrong? Of course, in every sense of the word. But by whose standards? Certainly not those of his peers. By their standards, the only thing wrong with the scenario was that a) he got caught, and b) her surprise appearance might have led her to discover what they too were doing away from home.

Okay, we're not talking about a society of Ward Cleavers here, but when you consider that chasing women is one of professional sports' most time-honored traditions, when you consider that women are attracted to athletes like white on rice and can be found in abundance, then you begin to see that the vigorous pursuit of females isn't a sign of moral depravity; it's just another symptom of the "itch," that driving need to show that you can do it all and have it all—and get away with everything.

Obviously, this leads to some very interesting questions about fidelity and morality, whether he's married or not. The fact is, most players can and do live two separate lives. A player can be completely in love with everything that represents "home," but he can also have those "special" women on the road, usually without ever violating his feelings for his wife, his family, everything that's part of his *real* world.

How? How can there be no guilt involved? How can men literally have women in every city on the road and still go home after a road trip as if nothing happened? A former teammate of mine had a rather profound way of looking at this: "What I do on the road has no effect on my marriage whatsoever, because I love my wife. You could say that even though my body keeps ending up in the wrong place, my heart is always in the *right* place." I'm not sure how much merit that would carry with his wife, but there are a lot of athletes who embrace and agree with his philosophy whole-heartedly.

This might be a good place to point out that these men are not generally sleazy characters, rabid wolves frothing at the mouth, or stereotypical "Rudolph Vaselino" types with their shirts open to here and more gold chains than Mr. T. No, these are, for the most part, your All-American, down-home country boys who are doing what most men might do when far from home and surrounded by women who keep throwing themselves at their feet. The difference is that unlike most men, ballplayers have the access, as well as that drive to take a shot at something different, and therein lies the thrill—another way to scratch the itch. It's one more way the athlete can exercise his ego, reaffirm his stardom, and play the grand ol' game that exists within the game he's *paid* to play.

There's another game of chance (chase a few) many rookies have endured in order to make the passage to becoming "one of the guys." The rookie turns over all his cash and credit cards to an appointed veteran and allows his teammates to get him drunk, blindfold him, and drive him to some out-of-the-way bar. His objective: to meet a woman, convince her to drive him back to the hotel, and then convince her to stay the night. Mind you, he does this with no money, no idea where he is, and under the watchful eye of no less than a dozen teammates who are more than willing to let him somehow stumble home in the dark should he fail his mission. It's more like a fraternity prank than a secret plot to ruin the lives of athletes and their families, and that's really all there is to it: it's just another game to be played. To be honest, the actual act of "getting laid" is almost after the fact. The real thrill is the fun, the chase, the stories you'll be able to tell, and the competitive drive to prove that you can get the job done. Again, it's a way to show that you can do it all *and* get away with it.

Now, some guys take this game more seriously than others. I know a group of pro football players who never leave home without what they call their "road kit," the contents of which are fairly mind boggling: small drills for drilling holes in hotel-room walls or doors so they can play Peeping Tom, two or three different types of vibrators, four or five various sex toys. And you just don't go on the road without your road kit, just like you don't go to the stadium without your equipment. The "fun" and inexpensive part for these jocks, especially in minor league baseball, is to hang around the hotel lobby watching for good-looking women to check in, maybe a pack of groupies that always follows the team or, if you're extremely lucky, a group of female flight attendants. Then you spend the rest of the day trying to figure out what rooms they're in, and how to get into those rooms. As the legend goes, if you latch onto young women of the groupie variety you're guaranteed a good time, because there's nothing they won't do for you. End up with a bunch of stewardesses and you've gone to heaven: the stories you tell won't bear the slightest resemblance to what really happens (which usu-ally amounts to two or three holes being drilled in a wall or a door and a good deal of male adolescent hysteria), but you sure will be able to entertain your teammates the next day.

Baseball has raised this brand of entertainment to an art form. There's a time-honored ritual that says if you have a roommate and you bring a girl back to your room, you either share or you let him watch. Of course, he's certainly free to step out of the room, but you'd be surprised at how many stay for the show. Sometimes a "show" is set up ahead of time: a player knows he'll be bringing someone to his room, and the closet will be full of four or five guys peeking through slats or around corners while the player and his unsuspecting friend do whatever. And there's no question that the sexual thrill derived from this is nothing compared to the exhilaration of being able to say that they pulled it off.

Granted, these things aren't happening every day in every hotel room across the nation, but there are rituals that exist on an even grander scale. For example, the "scouting system." Even during a game, if an attractive woman is within visual contact, you can be sure that everyone on the bench or in the dugout knows she's there. It's just like jungle drums. Then there's usually an unofficial queing system set in motion to see who "gets" her, who wins the right to send the club-house boy or the trainer into the stands with a note for her, something to the effect of "meet me at the flats bar after the game." The confidence level here is sky-high, and why not? Nine times out of ten, he isn't going to get turned down.

Aside from the fun-and-games aspect of all this, there's also a high degree of superstition involved when it comes to women. Most athletes are highly superstitious (wear the same T-shirt during a streak, eat the same things before a game, stand next to the same guy during the national anthem), and often, the prescription for bad luck is a good woman: You're in a slump? Go sleep with an ugly woman. Want to change your luck? Have sex with someone of another race. If it sounds crude, it is, but it's a very acceptable way to ward off the demons, according to the standard pro sports cure for performance illness.

Unfortunately for the athlete with a different standard of right and wrong, who for some reason just doesn't feel right about all of this, his options are somewhat limited. You see, there are rules to be followed, which, simply stated, go something like this: You're expected to love your wife, be a good provider, a good father, and all those things that being married and having children are all about. *But,* you're also expected to fit in with your peers, and to fit in you have to follow certain regulations and rituals, and sometimes one of those regulations and rituals happens to be chasing women. Anyone in pro sports will tell you he's seen more than one guy run out of town because he won't play along, because he makes his teammates uncomfortable. In this private society, if you want to make it, you play by the rules and adhere to traditions. The ones who don't conform to the social structure end up being washed out of the system before they even have a career.

Of course, the system will always tolerate the superstar, the hero who can do whatever he pleases because his competitive performance levels allow him that freedom. But the minute those performance levels drop below what is considered "acceptable," he's gone. If it sounds hypocritical, it is. But that's how it has always worked, and probably always will.

For the player who has no interest in cheating on

his wife or sleeping with strange women, the pressure put on him by his peers is phenomenal. It's somewhat similar to what a young woman goes through when her friends start becoming involved with men: Are you still a virgin? Are you not a virgin? Are you doing it? Are you not doing it? There's no place to hide. Everyone likes to feel that what he's doing is "okay," and it's threatening to see someone who doesn't agree with the way you live your life.

The only group of guys who can ignore the "life"—the partying, the drinking, the chasing—and get away with it is the born-again Christians. Hard-core Christianity makes it very acceptable to be straight, and you rarely see anyone put pressure on these players to "play along." But unless you're very serious about your religion, they'll never leave you alone.

Early in my major league career, I knew a guy who wanted to be a virgin when he got married. He was somewhat religious, but certainly not intense about it. For the four years we were teammates, absolutely everybody tried to get him laid. Everybody—the players, the coaches, the manager. They did everything they could to force a set of values on him that he couldn't accept, and he took endlessly painful abuse for it. Fortunately for him (and to everyone else's relief) he finally did get married, but he never did understand that just going out with the boys and being a good guy wasn't enough: the group has to see you leave with someone on occasion, or hear a war story or two, or else you have no credibility. This particular player managed to stay with the team as long as he did because he was an outstanding athlete, but he was fortunate. The bottom-line rule states expressly that there is no room for sensitivity or a truly moral approach to male-female relationships. It's just not acceptable behavior.

Now, we all know that these athletes are not in this alone—they're not attracting their female companions by clubbing them over their heads and dragging them, screaming, into hotel rooms against their will. No doubt many women find ballplayers and their attitudes to be somewhat repulsive, but many others are attracted to the so-called glamour and excitement associated with the sports world. There's an unfortunate stereotype about women who go out with athletes: that they're fortune-hunting, star-screwing "bimbos" who let themselves be used and abused by jocks who are more than willing to use and abuse them. In certain cases, you'll probably find this to be true, but on the whole, the women you see with athletes are perfectly normal people who know and understand exactly what they're getting into—because once a woman lets an athlete into her life, all sense of normalcy goes out the window—especially with the money involved in today's sports.

She soon finds out that she might be his favorite girl in the city she lives in, but that there might be a dozen others like her in major league cities across the country. She sees right away that she'll never come before his sport or his family. And she knows without a doubt that she's just another player in the game that's being played off the field. Why does she put up with it? Because, as one woman put it, "I knew without a doubt that this was a here-today-gone-tomorrow fling, but to be honest, I really didn't care. It was exciting, and sometimes you just don't want to say no."

Every woman who becomes involved with a married athlete goes through the painful reckoning that no matter how great their relationship might be, she's a welcome distraction throughout the season—and when his playing season has ended, so does the relationship. At the very best, she's put on hold, giving a whole new meaning to the concept of the "off-season." One woman I know learned this the hard way: "I was involved with a player who went crazy over me, and even though he was married, he brought me out in public, took me on the road with him, introduced me to all of his friends, bought me expensive gifts, treated me like a queen. Then the season ended, and it was as if my life ended with it. I believed then and I still believe today that he loved me, but once he headed home to his wife and family, it was as if I'd never existed. I heard from him once the entire off-season, and when the next season rolled around, guess who showed up with a dozen roses? I told him to hit the road, and I'm embarrassed to tell you that it was one of the toughest decisions I've ever had to make."

Saying no to athletes can be tough, simply because they don't know the meaning of the word. Think about it: how many people actually have the gall to say no to a sports star? A former stewardess I know once told me about the star she tried to say no to, despite the fact that he had followed her off their flight and up to her hotel room. Apparently they had hit it off on the flight, but when she found out he was married, she politely backed off and assumed that would be the end of it. Unfortunately, he refused to acknowledge her message, and two hours later he was still at her hotel-room door, serenading her and making up poems about why they should get together. Finally, mortified that everyone in the hotel was listening, she let him in the room to say, once again, "Thanks but no thanks." But before she could finish two sentences, he made himself comfortable and promised that he just really liked her, liked talking to her, and just wanted to be friends. She bought it. ("Not the smartest thing I've ever done," she admitted, "but he seemed fairly honest.") Somewhere during the polite conversation that followed, she excused herself to go to the bathroom, and returned to find her new friend lying stark naked on the bed.

"I didn't join him that night nor in the many months that followed, even though those months included countless midnight phone calls, expensive presents, plane tickets to various cities, and items that were generally mortifying but never actually surprising. Let's face it, once a man has hustled his way into your room and ripped off his clothes, it's hard to be surprised by anything.

"But I have to admit that although I still had no interest in him, there was something incredibly exciting about it. It was pretty clear that he took great pride in orchestrating his little plans, and he got so much pleasure out of playing this game that

I didn't have the heart to tell him to knock it off.

"In fact, I've met quite a few athletes through my work as a flight attendant—I've even dated a couple—and I can say without a doubt that although the faces, teams, and names change, they are essentially all the same. All of them, right down to the lines they use and the attitudes they take when you tell them you are or aren't interested. It's as if they've all read the same manual on how to seduce women. I've talked to other women I know who have been involved with jocks, and they agree: underneath it all, they're utterly, completely, thoroughly the same."

And still, knowing what it's like, would these women do it again? You bet. One woman put it this way: "I've had affairs with athletes that have gone on for years, and they're always difficult. You don't know if he's going to call, you never know whether you're going to see him. You have to learn to share him with the game, with his wife and kids, with other women. It's a no-win situation. Still, when I think of the places I've been able to go, the people I've been able to meet, the memories I have, I wouldn't trade my experiences for anything. The kind of excitement these guys carry around with them is a rare find—I feel lucky to have been a part of that world, even if only for a short time."

*   *   *   *

Now, somewhere out there, wondering what's going on, is the wife. She knows that during the season her husband is going to spend more time with his sports family—teammates, coaches, writers, fans—than with his nuclear family. She also knows that it's her duty to smile and deal with it, and that goes for the part of the life no wife wants to face: his life on the road.

"There's an automatic denial system built in," said one ex-wife who got out when she got tired of her husband's girlfriend calling their house and hanging up nightly. "We all suspect that someone else's husband is fooling around, but never our own. And the guys do such an incredible job of protecting each other that you'd probably never find out *anything* unless you were slapped in the face with it as I was. It's a shame they can't feel the same sense of loyalty to their own wives."

It's that same unwavering loyalty that prompts the typical clubhouse announcement on road trips: "Just want you guys to know that my wife's in town ... we're going to this restaurant and we're on that floor of the hotel, so if you're going out, go somewhere else." You hear that every night on a road trip whenever there's a wife within discovery distance. The fact remains that if you're the wife of a player, you too are bound by tradition to play by the rules, and Rule Number One states that the "real world" shalt not intrude on the sports world: when the two clash, it's guaranteed disaster.

Consider, for example, what happened one summer when a group of players' wives were to sponsor a celebrity softball game while their husbands were on the road, wives versus stars. Some unsuspecting moron let the wives into the clubhouse to get their husbands' jerseys, and each wife made a beeline straight to her husband's locker, that holy bastion of privacy and secrecy. It is a player's most personal place in the world, and here are thirty crazed wives, reading through love notes, searching through photos of half-clothed women, looking through lists of names and numbers he's collected. The net result of this real-world/sports-world encounter was three divorces and two separations. And while no player could justify why he actually had those letters and pictures and numbers, each held firm to the belief that the wives had trespassed on private property, and had overstepped their boundaries when they crossed over into forbidden territory.

But you can just imagine how the wives felt, finally being able to get a glimpse into that secret society and discovering that all their worst fears had been confirmed. As one wife later stated, "It's one thing to have a general fear and suspicion about what goes on when you're not around. But to actually see the proof makes the separation factor all that more terrifying."

Most wives know and accept that they must deal with the separation factor, as well as the fact that the rumors they hear about what goes on away from home just might involve their husband. "It's a horrible feeling," said one wife, still married to a ballplayer after eighteen years, "but you go along with it for the sake of his career. When our first child reached school age, we made the decision that I would remain at home in Florida until school was out for summer vacation. It was the first year I wouldn't be with him in the city he played in, and it terrified me for a number of reasons: One, who would look out for him when he needed moral support? And two, would he look for a replacement for me in another woman?

"The time we spent apart created horrible problems for our marriage. It was terribly lonely for me, since all the women I knew were either single looking for men, or married and going out with their husbands. I didn't fit into either group. My husband was going through similar experiences, and before long, he began to run with the group that was always looking for women. He became one of the boys, and the effect on our marriage was devastating. He went from a man I thought I knew and trusted to someone with total disregard for old-fashioned needs, commitment, fidelity, and responsibility. And the joke of it all was, his public image was still that of the squeaky clean All-American boy, the devoted family man and perfect husband. What a joke."

And yet she, like so many other wives, has stuck with it. Why? As the ex-wife put it, "They feel they've been through so much with him: the days when he was riding the bench, the days when the paper criticized everything he did, the days when he didn't know what city he'd been playing in. Then, once he's made it, she doesn't want to give up what she worked so hard to get: the fame, the money, the payoff. It's a lot to ask of someone to walk away from all of that. The fact that she's Mrs. So-and-so makes it a lot easier to take some of the garbage."

How else would you explain why one particular wife was willing to stay with her wandering husband after this little scenario: The ballplayer had made the incredibly dumb decision to fool around in the same city he lived in, and is strolling through a shopping mall with his girlfriend on his arm, killing time before a night game. As they walk into a store, they run right into his wife and mother-in-law. Most men might either faint or run, but this is a ballplayer, and for him, half the challenge is getting away with it, right? So he looks his wife straight in the eye and says, "Honey, are you going to believe me, or those lying eyes of yours?" They're still together, so she either chose to believe him (which isn't too likely) or she chose to grin and bear it.

Same attitudes, different couple: The jock goes out with the boys after the game, ends up going home with a woman he's just met, and finally manages to find his own house around dawn. He opens the door as quietly as possible, tiptoes down the hall, and there's his wife sitting on the stairs. Without missing a beat, he smiles at her from ear to ear and says, "Don't bother to call the police, I escaped." There was no way she bought the line, but she stayed with him, and it probably didn't hurt his cause that he was a superstar earning major dollars.

I'm certainly not suggesting that all players' wives stay with their husbands because of their stardom and money, because there are a lot of professional athletes who never attain any great amount of either. But the percentage of divorce among athletes *after* their retirement is astronomical—42 percent—compared with 30 percent of athletes who get divorced during their playing days. The issue here is that as long as an athlete is making the money and riding the wave of success, his wife at least has a reason to overlook the infidelity, the running around, and the deception. She'll most likely never *accept* it, but she may be able to justify, in her own mind, why she should stay with him.

The sad truth is that as long as there has been professional sports, there have been superego athletes who know that because of their glamorous image, they can run with whomever they want, whenever they want. That's not ever going to change. Interestingly, even in this era of sexual caution, most athletes turn their heads from the warnings of AIDS. Many teams in several sports have offered voluntary AIDS testing, and no more than 17 percent of all the players who could have been tested even bothered to take the test. The attitudes you hear range from "Well, if I've got it, I've got it . . . what's a test going to tell me?" to "Hey, I never had sex with a guy, how'm I gonna get AIDS?" The fact remains that while you do hear some jocks saying, "I don't want to die for a piece of ass even though I feel like killing for one," you have the same denial systems at work here that apply to all other facets of an athlete's life: I'll never get old, I'll always be in the game, I'll always be good-looking, I'll never get AIDS. It's the same philosophy that leads him to cheat on his wife, take advantage of other women, party hard, and still be able to perform on the field; he believes that his life has been charmed, that nothing bad could ever happen to him, and that no matter what, people will always love and accept him because he's a superior creature. Sadly, he'll never believe otherwise until he leaves the game and suddenly discovers that his wife might not put up with the same crap, that the women have turned their attention toward "bigger" names, and that his star might not be shining so brightly anymore. And now he begins to play the toughest game of all, trying to make it in the *real* world, where his formerly acceptable values are completely unacceptable.

4
Husbands and Fathers

I f you took two seventeen-year-olds, a jock and a homecoming queen, got them married, gave them $400,000 a year, and put them in a situation where they were highly visible across the nation, how do you think they'd make out when the cash disappeared and the lights went out?

Welcome to the Baseball Marriage.

If you accept the notion that athletes are indeed terminally adolescent—physically adult but mentally juvenile—then you're asking a newly married ballplayer to do what no teenager could ever do: accept the responsibilities of marriage.

When these kids say "I do," they're accepting an entirely different set of values from what most people live by, agreeing to a marriage that will require them to do things and cope with things that other newlyweds their age will never have to deal with. Consider the fact that he will spend more time with his teammates than he will with his wife and children throughout his entire career. Add to this the fact that he will literally be away from home for two-thirds of the year, a strain which would test even the best marriage. The fact that the terminally adolescent athlete most likely lacks the maturity to handle such a situation makes it virtually impossible for such a marriage to survive.

Let's first establish the fact that most ballplayers are married. There are some single guys, but they're usually young and usually married by their second or third season in the big leagues.

And when you think about the mentality of the ballplayer, it's no mystery why so many are married. First, he's not particularly good at fending for himself, either domestically or financially. He's always had a mother or father for that, and now he'll have a wife to take care of things like laundry, cooking, and balancing a checkbook: ballplayers usually can't do any of the above. Second, he needs the support system, the cheering section, the ego boost, that his family provided when he was younger, and now his wife can take their place. It's her role as the wife of a ballplayer, and it might be one of the toughest jobs on the face of the earth. I don't mind when my daughters date athletes, but I sure hope they don't marry them.

Most players marry early, either as minor leaguers, or rookies, and it is almost always the prototypical homecoming queen/princess/cheerleader types they choose. And while their careers are going well, so are their marriages. Plenty of status, plenty of flash, enough money to survive (or at least the promise of enough to survive), lots of posturing, playing at being married, playing at buying houses, playing at having children, playing at living, much the same as they played their games on the field and off the field before they got married.

Most of these marriages are doomed to failure unless one or the other, or hopefully both, of the individuals become aware of the fact that relationships must be *worked* at, and that marriage is not a win-win situation. Anybody can be on top of the world. Anybody can be visible and make lots of money, drive a Mercedes, wear diamonds, and all those fun things, and still hold a marriage together. It's when the bad times come that the substance of the marriage becomes important. If there is no substance there, the marriage is not going to work.

Most ballplayers love their wives dearly, but don't necessarily like their wives, especially when the game gets shaky and the career nears an end. Remember, while a player is living out his fantasy, his wife has had to cope, has had an opportunity to grow up, usually before her husband is ready to do the same thing. Typically, they met while he was in the minor leagues, and they're both small-town kids. The big leagues can do a lot to show a boy the ways of a fantasy world. He's traveling across the country staying in great hotels and eating in fancy restaurants and meeting fast-track men and glamorous women. The wife? She's back at home, learning to anchor the relationship, learning about re-

sponsibility, providing stability, and hoping
nothing has really changed. Oh, they have more
money to spend and more public appearances to
make, but *she* hasn't changed the way her husband
has. He's becoming more sophisticated (although
not necessarily more mature), and before long, his
wife decides she doesn't want to move along with
him in his "new" world. You hear ballplayers say
about their wives, "She just hasn't come to party in
the big leagues. She still thinks like a minor
leaguer." Translation from her point of view: She's
happy for but not impressed by his flashy friends
and glitzy lifestyle. She'd be just as happy if he'd
find a few more hours with family, a little more
time to spend with her and the kids.

What do baseball players expect their wives to
be? They expect their wives to be everything that
their baseball team, players' association, agents,
and parents can't be for them. It's a rough role:
she's supposed to act and look like a ballplayer's
wife, but she can *never* be a part of the inner
sanctum of her husband's world. She can do the
wives' club things, she can do community service,
and she can look real good at his side on the ban-
quet circuits, but she's not allowed any crossover
into clubhouse matters or team politics and she'll
never hear about what happens on the road. Occasionally, however, a rogue wife will break out of
the "hold."

There is such a thing as a "bad" baseball wife,
and sometime, on every team, someone gets traded
or released because of his wife.

What is a bad wife? A bad wife is someone who

sits in the stands and criticizes other players, the manager, or coaches or complains about the front office. She's more visible and vocal than many of the others. Her status as a wife is usually the result of what her husband is doing on the field, and when she starts to use that status to elevate herself above the other wives, it's a problem. A bad wife is also someone who talks about what she *knows* goes on during road trips with *other* husbands, or tells the press her husband should have more playing time, or chews out another wife for *her* husband's lousy error or strikeout. There have been some major clubhouse explosions over a player's inability to control his wife's mouth and attitude.

This is only surpassed by having the wrong *ex*-wife. It's bad enough when the player has to deal with his ex, but when the whole organization has to deal with her, that player may become more trouble than he's worth. Maybe she knows secrets about other players, or maybe her lawyers are harassing the front office over the size of his contract. Whatever, it's bad news.

How about watching a player try to dodge a court summons? You have guys sleeping at the ballpark avoiding hotels and airports, to avoid being served with divorce papers. Thank God for the sanctity of "Only Ballplayers" in the clubhouse.

Not that he doesn't deserve what he gets, or that she doesn't deserve what she's asking for. Wives really pay their dues, especially when it comes to family living and children. I look back on what I went through with the minor leagues, being on a yo-yo back and forth between the minors and the majors. How many times did I just jump on a plane and take off to meet a ball club somewhere, leaving Karren and the kids behind to get out of leases, pack up the Volkswagen bus, hit the freeway, and drive down to whatever city we were playing in just to be there after we came off a road trip?

The time is *now* in professional baseball. When you're in Triple-A or Double-A and the call comes through from the parent club that says "Come up here and get here quick," you jump on a plane and go, regardless of what it puts your wife and children through.

My first year in the big leagues, I went back and forth four times between Richmond and Atlanta, and we physically moved from apartment to apartment three of the four times.

Wives do a lot of those things by themselves. I was very fortunate that two of my three children were born during winter months when I could be home. When my son was born, I was in Cleveland. I read about it on the scoreboard, sprinted in from the bullpen, and called on a stadium pay phone to find out if my wife and son were all right.

It's a little different today. Most teams allow a player to go home for a birth, but it sure wasn't something that was done on a regular basis ten to fifteen years ago. Sorry, Mrs. Ballplayer, you're on your own.

The thing to remember about any professional baseball career is that, for all intents and purposes, the career comes first. It's a very unusual player who puts family ahead of career, no matter what he says. It's a difficult balance to achieve between

the two. You feel like you must commit 100 percent
to your career, even though you want to do the
same for your family. It must be similar to any
occupation that requires a commitment beyond a
nine-to-five job, whether it be that of an airline
pilot or an entertainer.

Not surprisingly, a baseball wife finds herself
with conflicting feelings about her husband and
his career. She loves him and she loves the pay-
check, but she hates the sport and the way it keeps
him from her.

It's not that she doesn't like the people; she *does*
like the people. And it's not because she doesn't like
the game itself. But she doesn't like what the game
and its people force her husband to do, including
the travel time away from the family, commitments
to the field, late-night phone calls, long absences,
winter ball during the off-season, all the things
that enter into the blind willingness of an athlete
trying to stay in the big leagues. The family and the
relationship go on the back burner.

Consider, too, the daily fear she faces—fear of
his being injured, being traded, being released, not
to mention other women on the road. She's seen it
all happen to other wives: one day you're the toast
of the town, the next day you're invisible. That's the
reality of it. It's an incredibly insecure existence,
made tolerable by the false sense of security created by the success and fame. When those start to
fade—or, even worse, when they're suddenly
yanked away—both husband and wife go down
together.

Most divorces (almost half of all baseball marriages end in divorce) occur postcareer, within eighteen months after a guy has left the game. There are several reasons for this. First, the husband is going to have identity problems: who am I, what am I, why am I; he's wrangling with self-conflict, self-confidence, and self-esteem. But on the flip side, his wife, who is trying to offer all the love and support that she should be able to give her husband in a career crisis, is suddenly resentful over the fact that he has been released from the game. She's just as angry at him for getting released as he is at himself and the people who released him.

It's the toughest time of a player's life, and certainly the most stressful on his marriage. Baseball economics is based on the principle of "have a better year, make more money, spend more money." Then you get released and your earning curve drops significantly. The high profile drops significantly. Everything that relates to your fast-paced existence stops abruptly. There is resentment—deep-set resentment—covered up under the guise of "pseudosupport." There is no couple I've known, no marriage I've known, that didn't suffer on both sides when the guy got released.

If being a baseball husband is tough, being a baseball father is incredibly frustrating. I understand now why my wife used to say, "You don't know what you're missing. You have no idea what these children are all about. You come in and play the Band-Aid game. Anyone can be nice to a kid for three months. When you grind it with them day in

and day out, they get to be a pain in the ass. You
don't know them and they don't really know you."
I completely missed the growing up of my oldest
daughter. I came home one winter and said to her,
"Let's pop on down to the market." She said, "Okay,
Dad, I'll drive." And I said, "You can't drive. You
don't have your license."

She answered, "Come to the party, Dad. I got my
license three months ago."

I did a little bit better with my middle daughter
because she was still pretty young when I got released as a player, and so I spent more time at
home.

I am doing a lot better with my son. Both with
the San Diego Padres and with the Texas Rangers,
I have actually taken him with me for the summer.
When he gets out of school in June, he becomes my
roommate. It hasn't been easy, especially when he
was six or seven years old and had to be watched in
the clubhouse while the game was going on. There
have been some embarrassing moments, but I am
very thankful for the patience of both the Rangers
and the Padres in allowing me to be a real parent
during the season.

Would I want my son to be a professional baseball player? If I can do for my son all the things
that I think need to be done to prepare a child for
life, then I would not mind at all if he had a baseball career that he could get enjoyment out of. He
likes to play baseball. He is good at it. He understands the environment.

But I won't be horribly disappointed if he

doesn't play professional baseball. I hope he continues to be good at sports and enjoys them. Maybe even get his college education paid for by a University that could use his academic and athletic talent, or that he's rewarded with something other than just getting sweaty. If he *did* end up in professional baseball, I would only be happy if he had the *life skills* to match up to his *baseball skills*. And if that were to happen, Bryan would undoubtedly be one of the lucky few who could boast such a gift.

It's easy to be objective once you're out of the game. The truth is, most players don't even *know* their kids well enough to suggest what they should do with their lives. More likely, a player returns home in October, sees that everyone still lives there, and marvels at how his kids have grown so much.

Here is where a good baseball wife comes into the picture. If he's lucky, he's married to someone who understands him and the game; she can often carry the load during those times when he's gone. She knows it's her job, but could you blame her for feeling like a single parent?

It's a strange scenario: As an athlete, he can't be beat; he just naturally succeeds at everything he does. But as a husband, success doesn't come quite as naturally. The best way to describe him is that he's very long on intentions and extremely weak on follow-through. He works *around* situations instead of working *with* situations.

He's completely willing to go to any lengths to keep Mom and the kids happy with houses, cars, clothes, toys, and all the trappings, but has a very difficult time giving of himself, opening up, sharing and communicating, getting involved with the family. His nature dictates his limited emotions, and the only emotions that he can allow himself— the only feelings he is comfortable with—are anger and aggression; that's all he's programmed to know. The soft side of most professional athletes doesn't come to the surface very often. It's a muscle that they're simply not used to flexing.

Such a relationship may be workable when things are going well, but when a marriage goes bad or fights occur or separations get to be too much, it's rarely—in the player's opinion—*his* fault. He's sure that he's giving everything he is capable of giving to the relationship, and he can't really understand why his wife says, "You're not giving me what I need to make this marriage go." He can't compute this: isn't he still the star ballplayer? His fans still love him, so what's *her* problem? All anyone has ever asked of him is to win, and that's fine with him. He's the chronic terminal adolescent: a man who is still emotionally fifteen or sixteen years old in his approach to interpersonal relationships. He is not a bad person, just an *unskilled* person when it comes to fulfilling the traditional role of being a husband and father.

But this isn't always acceptable to his wife and kids, who don't care about him as an athlete, only as a man they need in their lives. Meanwhile, he believes he *is* in their lives—he can't understand what they're upset about. You hear many players say, "My family means everything to me. I can go home to them and forget the oh-for-four or the errors. They're always there for me." One question: Can they say the same of him?

Ballplayers are extremely good at playing a game when they know the rules. Unfortunately, the relationship game doesn't come with a rule book. For many athletes, it's the one game they don't win often enough.

5
On the Road Again

Imagine you have a job that takes you out of town for half of every month, at the very least. You stay in nice hotels, and you don't actually have to go to work until four in the afternoon. Sounds nice, right? Now imagine how you'd fill the hours. Oh, at first it's fun to check out new places and cities, but let's be honest—how many times can you go adventuring in Pittsburgh?

You can admire a ballplayer for his talents, for his wealth, for his fame. But don't *ever* admire his having the "privilege" to get away from home and travel. It is definitely not one of the high points of playing baseball. Does it get lonely on the road? Do players mind road trips? How often does a wife make a road trip? How often does she go on the road with her husband, or how often does a girl-friend go on the road with her ball-playing boy-friend? And are women welcomed by teammates, or are they a hindrance because they get that rare glimpse at what is actually going on?

Baseball is kind of like the army: it's hurry up and wait, pass the time until the battle. Win enough battles and you win the war. There are both personal and team battles to be fought, and the baseball existence includes downtime and up-time, both at home and on the road. Neither is easy, but for an athlete, being on the road is much tougher than being at home. In fact, you spend half your career trying to get by mentally, emotionally, and physically on road trips. Now, if you believe everything you hear, you probably imagine a bunch of unleashed jocks rampaging through unsuspecting cities, finally free from the wife and kids and loving every minute. For some I'm sure that's true, but for most, that's a myth. You can itemize "downtime" into a number of categories ranging from the tedious to the titillating.

On the more tedious end of the scale you have the card games: spades, hearts, casino, pluck. These are the easier games, pastimes of some of the not-so-bright athletes. The brighter guys, the ones who want to be challenged a little bit more, will play bridge, pinochle, whist, or cribbage. Gambling is the common denominator between the bright and the not-so-bright. The gambling runs the gamut; you name the game and gamblers will be playing it.

Then there are crossword puzzles, chess, backgammon, and checkers, activities where you find another cross section of people. The brighter guys will work the *New York Times* crossword puzzle, and the slower ones will work the puzzle in the local paper. You see guys playing chess, using those little magnetized chessboards, especially on the planes. Backgammon, a fashionable thing to do for a while, is still played, but not with the intensity it once was. The real slow guys, the double-digit IQ guys, play checkers.

It never fails: ballplayers play these games with the same intensity that they play baseball. You can bet the farm that the guy who goes berserk on the field when he strikes out is the same guy who sends checkers flying all over the room when he loses. A guy who can't stand to lose can't stand to lose anytime, to anyone, whether the game is baseball or Crazy Eights. The new distraction is video games. A big-league ball club consists of twenty-four adult children, and they hit the video arcade with a vengeance. In Cleveland's Bond Court Hotel (and God bless Cleveland, but there is not a whole lot to do in that city), ballplayers will conservatively spend $50 to $100 in an afternoon before a ball game trying to maximize their scores, and competing with each other to become Masters of the Universe.

Then there's the time-passing category that I would call nonbaseball sports. Here you're talking mainly golf, which is very big with some organizations and not allowed by others, but even when it's not allowed guys still play. Baseball players love to play golf because it's a sport that's played early in the day. You can still get home, have a bite to eat, take a nap, and gear up for a ball game.

There is always the swimming pool and sunbathing, a category for passing time that has ramifications in other parts of baseball life: wherever there is sun, you get females in bathing suits. Enough said.

Ballplayers fall victim to a syndrome that causes them to stay up late at night and then sleep late in the morning. Your whole day is shifted six to eight hours from a normal day for the rest of the world; keeping normal hours on the road is very, very difficult. When you're at home with the wife and children, they get up at 7:30 or 8:00 in the morning, even when they stayed up late the night before to watch your game. So they force you to get up and get your body moving. If you don't watch yourself when you are on the road, you become not just a couch potato but a bed potato. You will actually, in effect, change your body clock until you're on the same split shift that a factory worker would experience.

Players try to deal with this in different ways. Depending on how many time zones away from home you are, you can try to live by your watch; leave it set on "home time," and eat and sleep at the same times you would if you were at home. This does help keep your body clock from being screwed up, but it does have its problems, especially when you live in the east, travel to the west, and find yourself trying to eat lunch at nine in the morning. You do your best.

Other guys believe that staying busy is the way to cope with life on the road, so they look for ways to alleviate boredom, to keep them occupied, and there are some classics. For example, I know one guy who has been unbelievably successful at going into a city and wandering around the financial districts, going to a bank and locating the "pick of the litter" of the female tellers. Then he goes up and tries to cash an out-of-state check for $1,000, from his account back home. Translation: "I need to cash this check because I'm important and need to do some important things." The woman finds out that he's a ballplayer and that he has $1,000 in his pocket.

It doesn't matter whether he spends it or not: the goal is to meet this cute little thing who's helped him cash his check and then thank her by leaving her some tickets for the ball game, or asking her out to lunch and seeing where it goes from there. It's really a lounge lizard approach in a banking environment. But the success rate is pretty solid.

Surprisingly, in today's game, more players bring children and wives and/or girlfriends on road trips. It's much more acceptable than it was when I signed twenty years ago. In fact, it was taboo twenty years ago. Our organization, the Texas Rangers, allows you, twice a year, to bring your wife and kids on a chartered flight to a city of your choice and the ball club will actually pick up the tab. The rest of the time, there is really no limit to how often your family can travel with you, at your expense, and a lot of the guys, especially the newly married with no children, will have their wives with them quite a bit during the season.

Girlfriends will show up quite often also. Back when the money wasn't quite as big as it is today, a guy had to develop female contacts in every city he went to, if that's how he chose to spend his time. Now, things being what they are, and people being a little bit more cosmopolitan and able to afford plane tickets, players will actually fly their girl-friends with them.

The only aspect that has never changed is what happens in the clubhouse before everyone's head-ing off to go out and do their thing after a ball game. The guys who have girlfriends or wives and children will alert everybody about where they're going to be, so the hounds can go somewhere else and not be seen by hometown folk. Then you just pray that your teammate's visiting wife—who happens to be *your* wife's best friend—doesn't see you walking into the hotel elevator with a strange female.

There is another specialized boredom alleviator, called "dialing for dollars," "call the world," or "black cord fever." This occurs when you come back with a snootful, you're a little hammered, and you slide into your room and pick up the phone and start calling. You don't realize until you go to check out of the room just how much you spent on black cord fever. I've seen guys who have had bills of four hundred or five hundred dollars for three days in one city. And they have no idea who they called.

Then, of course, there's "dialing for Domino's." You know, "Domino's Pizza delivers," just like in the commercial. It's always the heavy-duty guys— the big thumpers, the wide-body guys—who have the tendency to come back after a game and order four or five large pizzas, two or three six-packs, and sit up watching HBO or ESPN. While they're watching the world badminton championships, they devour the whole mess. I'm basically an early riser, and on my way out for an early-morning jog, I'm liable to be bowled over by the smell of pepperoni or anchovy pizzas before I'm even near the room. You don't sleep with pizza boxes in your room, of course; as soon as you finish with the box, whether you ate all the pizza or not, it goes right outside the door for the maids to pick up in the morning.

Maybe a final category for specialized boredom alleviators would be the room-service blues. That's where you get back, and you have had a good night or a bad night, and you're by yourself. You don't feel like doing this, you don't feel like doing that, so you pull out the room-service menu and pick and choose whatever will make you feel right.

There are variations on that theme. One of the better stories I've heard happened in New York, where if you order room service, it's going to cost you $35 for a Coke and a hamburger.

This guy called down and ordered a twenty-eight-course meal and had it delivered to his room. He let the waiter in, and let him do his thing—spread the wings out, set the table, the whole works. In the interim, he had nuded up. When the startled waiter tried to hand him the check to sign, the player slammed him against the wall, then told him to stay there and not move. He then sat down on the bed and, stark naked, proceeded to literally shove food in his face, occasionally tossing a roll or chicken bone or two at the terrified waiter.

This is what road trips can do to a man.

6
What Baseball Doesn't Want You to Know

I f there's one thing baseball loves, even more than warm weather for postseason play, it's self-promotion. There is no other sport that operates such a tireless PR machine, cranking out statistics and stories and image builders all over the place. This is the National Pastime, after all— gotta look the part.

But there is one thing that baseball, like all public image professions, must keep quiet about— family business. Words to live by: if it happened behind the scenes, let it *stay* behind the scenes.

Baseball protects its own, no matter what the offense, as long as the offense stays within the confines of the baseball world. You may have a serious gambling problem, and the team may know about it, but they'll keep your secret as long as you perform, and as long as you keep your problem to yourself. Someone may take you aside and tell you to watch yourself, but no one is going to talk to the press or the commissioner's office until you do something to warrant it. Translation: Keep your nose clean and we'll take care of you. A double bind for players with problems.

It's hard to imagine how anything in sports can be secret anymore, particularly with the media always starved for a good scandal, but there are many things that baseball manages to keep quiet about. In fact, players who are foolish enough to discuss what went on in a closed clubhouse meeting, or reveal that two players almost killed each other after the game, often turn up on other teams the next year. That kind of behavior just isn't acceptable. You must be loyal to your teammates, even though you may hate every last one of them.

One year I played on a team that was making a run for a pennant for the first time in four or five years. One player, who was near the end of his career but was having a great season, asked for the night off.

The manager said, "Sure, you can have the night off, but I'll tell you what. After the game, I don't want to see you in the hotel lobby, I don't want to see you in the bar, I don't want to see you *anywhere*. You can sit on the bench and watch the game, and then you call it a night. If you take the night off, you *really* take the night off, get yourself some sleep, and come back pounding tomorrow."

So after the game, the player planned to settle in for the night; he even asked the trainer for some muscle relaxants, fully intent on doing exactly what the skipper had told him to do.

Well, after the ball game, our player did as he promised, and went back to his room to crawl in bed. But an hour later, about midnight, there was a tap-tap-tap on the door, and there stands his roommate with a woman he had picked up.

"Hey," said the roommate, "could you go for a walk for an hour or so, maybe a couple of hours, and give me a chance to get one-on-one with this lady here?"

And, being an accommodating fellow, the half-asleep player said, "Sure. See ya."

Having taken the muscle relaxants, he was fairly groggy, and decided he'd better keep a low profile, since he had promised the manager he would behave. So he just walked outside and began wandering around the parking lot. And that's where he was, sitting on one of the curb stoppers, when the manager comes strolling along, about fifteen minutes after curfew, with a snout full of cocktails.

Now, the player knows he's innocent, that he had indeed gone in early and did what he was supposed to do, and that under certain circumstances, ballplayers have an obligation to take care of each other, which was why he had gone for a walk while his roommate did his thing, and which was why he was out in the parking lot. Innocently.

This all makes perfect sense to the ballplayer, who opens his mouth to explain to the manager, but is cut short because the manager basically comes unglued. Red face, veins popping out, the works. They go face to face.

"You son of a bitch, you no-good asshole!" screams the manager. The player, confident he is right, and more confident that the manager is totally smashed, says, "Well, let's not argue about it here in the parking lot. Let's go back to your room and we'll get this thing ironed out." And off they stumble, one drunken skipper and one half-asleep ballplayer on muscle relaxers.

Well, about forty-five minutes later, the whole team is in the manager's room trying to break these two guys up. They were like a couple of bull elks going at each other. You could hear it all over the hotel: doors breaking down, lamps smashing, everybody rushing out of their rooms trying to keep these two from murdering each other. It was a pretty tense night.

The next day at the ballpark, we looked like we had just returned from the Revolutionary War. Everybody had at least one black eye, puffed-up lips, scraped elbows, and sore hands. It had been a real knockdown battle.

The skipper called everybody together. "All right," he said, "we got everything ironed out last night. It's over. But we gotta come up with a story for the media, because we don't exactly look like any oil painting right now." The team pulls together and comes up with a story that we got involved in a game that got a little carried away, and some of the guys took friendly beatings accordingly.

The point is that you're loyal to each other because you are a *team*, and even though you may not be happy with what is going on, you would be less happy if the story was told outside the team. In this case, the whole group pulled together when it had to, and presented a united front, not only to the media but to the opposing ball clubs and to the outside world.

A similar thing happened to me a few years later when my team was on a West Coast road trip. It was a Saturday night; I was slated to pitch on Sunday. I'm in my room, sound asleep, when the phone rings. The hostess from the hotel bar (where I had been earlier) is calling to say, "One of the writers is down here passed out. Is there any possibility that you could come down and get him up to his room?" I know she's calling me because she doesn't really know anyone else connected to the team, and, like a nice guy, I say, "Okay, sure. I'll come down."

So I go down, pick him up, drag him back to his room, fish his key out of his pocket, push him inside the door, lay him out on the bed, make sure he's alive, and return to my room.

About forty-five minutes later, after the bar has closed, the phone rings again and it's the hostess at the bar saying, "Can you come on back down? That writer has left his wallet and charge cards down here."

Now I'm getting a little irritated, but I say, "Okay, yeah, I'll come down." So I go down and pick them up, and I'm walking out of the bar, thinking I'm finally going to get some sleep, when along comes one of the owners of our ball club, with the general manager, the field manager, and one of the coaches. And there I stand in front of the elevator.

Needless to say, the skipper, whose bosses are right behind him, comes after me like a barracuda.

I really wasn't in any position to make him understand my story; he just told me that if I didn't win the next day, that for all intents and purposes he'd kick my ass, fire me and/or release me, and not necessarily in that order.

So all night long I stared at the ceiling, wondering how in the hell I was going to explain, knowing he was drunk, probably pissed off, and definitely embarrassed that his starting pitcher was loitering in the lobby after curfew.

As it turned out, thank God, I went out and had one of the best starts (of my few starts) in my major league career—won the ball game, but it wasn't enough to get me off the hook. Afterward, the manager called me into his office and proceeded to read me the riot act.

I said, "Okay, Skip, let me tell you what really happened and you can do what you want to do." And I told him the story, and while he certainly didn't apologize point-blank, the true story got to the owner and general manager real fast. About five or six days later, there appeared in my locker a gift certificate for five hundred dollars at a local clothing store.

These are things you never read about. Even when members of the media are involved, even when the front office is involved, even when field personnel are involved, you'll never hear about these things; the inner workings of the baseball environment remain secret. Keep family business within house and deal with it accordingly. Baseball takes care of its own, period.

The media play an interesting role in all of this,

because they sure see a hell of a lot more than they could ever write. And in this age of full disclosure (i.e. printing every last dirty detail you can dig up), it's a miracle that the sports pages aren't packed daily with scandal, outrage, and mayhem.

But there's a strange dance that takes place between players and the press. Writers need the cooperation of players, for quotes and stories and for something to write about. Players need writers, for exposure and image-building and for a way to let the public know why they swung at that 3-and-0 pitch. They need each other. So even though many players look at writers as obnoxious, overweight jock-sniffers, and most writers look at athletes as moronic, unbred, uncivilized threats to society, they all smile and do their jobs. It's a matter of survival.

Therefore, all of those nasty secrets that media people observe—the owner's daughter caught sneaking out of the pitcher's room, the star who has to take a day off because his hangover is making him see triple—remain secret, not because the media feel an obligation to protect our sports heroes, but because the media feel an obligation to protect their relationship with those stars. Destroy the relationship, destroy your access.

It's a difficult relationship to maintain. Many athletes make it hard on themselves, either because they can't deal with the press, or they won't deal with the press. They might be articulate, witty people, but for some reason, they view the press as an intrusion and therefore can't bring themselves to cooperate. That's certainly their right, but can you blame the reporter on deadline for getting pissed off? It becomes cyclical: player won't talk, writer won't write about him, player becomes annoyed that writer never gives him any ink or poison pens him, ignores writer further, and so on.

There are good media people and bad, and the bad ones account for much of the reason why some players won't deal with the press. The athletes who have the most difficulty with the media are the ones who have difficulty communicating with just about anyone, either because of language barriers or personality barriers; some people just can't bring themselves to communicate. They simply *won't* communicate, maybe because they had a bad experience where they spilled their guts and then got in trouble for it, or maybe they got burned by a writer who told something he wasn't supposed to tell. Good media people will tell you that they're not out to get anyone, they just want to tell the story, but ballplayers have a hard time understanding that all reporters are not alike.

These "friendly" adversaries know they must peacefully coexist if either is going to survive, so in most cases, everyone puts on a happy face and endures. But it's interesting to see how the two groups, players and media, view each other.

Players break down the media into three different groups: writers, radio people, and television people. Writers are often seen as being a little sneaky, a little slovenly, a little out of shape, and a little on the drunken end of drinking. Radio people often appear as clueless, faceless voices that ask uninformed, silly questions (again and again), and who pass out restaurant gift certificates to players who appear on their shows. But they're usually harmless, and since most of them are affiliated with the ball club in some way, it's hard for them to say nasty things about the players. Television broadcasters are generally viewed as walking egos with blue blazers and more makeup than Tammy Bakker, who have all the answers to the questions before they ask them. Their priorities are, in this order, first making themselves look good, then noticing the play or the player.

On the other hand, you have the media people who don't exactly view athletes with loving kindness. Says one such writer:

"Players are big blobs of ego. Whether it's necessary or whether it just comes with the uniform I don't know, but when you're a player, people want to hear what you have to say; newspapers, magazines, TV, radio, the whole gamut. All I can say is that one of these days, they pay. When you're an ex-player, nobody cares. Those five-hundred-dollar fees for autograph sessions are nonexistent, and you almost have to commit a crime to get back in the news. It's a tough, bitter comedown, but it almost balances out the way that they act while they're at the top of their game."

Another comment, one that sums up the whole experience:

"I don't dislike ballplayers, even the assholes. Their attitudes are part of the clubhouse atmosphere and part of the system; they behave the way baseball has programmed them to behave.

"The truth is, they have their job to do and we

have ours. They play ball, we write about it. Whatever they do off the field, behind the scenes, isn't our responsibility to write about. That's their private business. And anyway, how much cooperation am *I* going to get when I need a quote from the same guy I wrote something rotten about the day before?"

You cannot separate baseball from the media or the media from baseball. They have a symbiotic relationship. What the average fan perceives, even the fan who goes to the ballpark, he still perceives players as they are reflected through the media. And it's a timeworn baseball tradition that dictates that the media shalt not violate the sanctity of the secretive side of the game.

*   *   *   *

One of the most rigidly observed ethical, moral, and traditional rituals has to do with a man's locker. It's his. Stay away. Just as there is honor among thieves, so is there honor among teammates, and no matter how well meaning you are, no matter what your reasons, there is *no* rationalization for going into someone else's locker without his permission.

It's amazing how open athletes are about their possessions. Every player has a "valuable box" in the clubhouse, and players will put their money clips, their watches, and their rings in their valuable box. But just as often, those items are left in pants pockets or on the top shelf of a locker, in plain view of the rest of the team. And we're not talking about five or ten bucks, we're talking about a money clip with three or four hundred dollars and a ten-thousand-dollar Rolex and World Series rings and whatever.

It's just an unspoken rule, albeit a strictly enforced rule: you don't steal from your teammates; you don't go in your teammates' lockers.

Lockers are probably the most graphic indicator of an athlete's personality. You can walk into the clubhouse, look around the lockers, and figure out the emotional makeup of every player. You can spot the guys who were potty trained too early—everything is in its place and there is a place for everything. And you can point to the scatterbrained guys, whose lockers look like they were organized with the help of a bomb.

And there, presiding over this bastion of holiness, is the unsung hero, the clubhouse man. Without this guy, I believe, baseball as we know it would cease to exist. I doubt any ball club could field a full team without the clubhouse man to get them there.

Clubhouse men manage the clubhouse, if not the team. They are responsible for getting bags from the airport—players' bags, athletic bags—to the clubhouse, unpacking gloves, shoes, uniforms, and so forth, so everything is ready to go when an athlete shows up at the ballpark.

A player may go through two complete sets of uniforms and undergarments a day, especially in a hot place like Texas and especially when there are double workouts, so there are washing machines and dryers right in the clubhouse, and there's the clubhouse man, washing and drying. In effect, clubhouse men become like mothers for players who aren't married and like wives for players who are. Except you get the feeling that no mother or wife on earth would put up with the amount of work generated by ballplayers. You have to wonder what most ballplayers live like at home, because they will come in off the field and start peeling clothes, and wherever those clothes come off is where they're going to lie until the clubhouse man picks them up.

It's amazing how fast a player can get used to the comforts of the clubhouse. When a guy first gets to the big leagues, he will walk clear across the clubhouse to get a can of tobacco or a can of Coca-Cola and not think twice. Within a month, if there's a clubhouse kid within shouting distance, the athlete will sit in his chair and say, "Hey, Clubbie, go get me this, go get me that."

The clubhouse guy is responsible for the Gatorade, the Cokes, the beer for after the ball game, and the snacks—anything from candy to fruit, depending on how nutritionally oriented the clubhouse guy might be. And he is responsible for some semblance of a meal after the ball game.

A clubhouse meal can be a religious experience. Or hell on earth. My eleven-year-old son travels with me during the summer, and one of the things he just can't get used to is watching a full four-course meal be insanely devoured after a ball game, by athletes in various states of undress, various states of mind, as they inhale chicken or fling potato salad at each other. The only rule is that you can't come near the food naked, a condition commonly described as "cock in the cooler" or "dick in the spread." Whatever you want to call it, you're not supposed to do it. Classy joints, these clubhouses.

Aside from that, anything goes. You watch guys eat and scratch and do all the things that they do as gross human beings, and all of this is going on while you're trying to eat. Nothing is sacred. In some of the older ballparks, Detroit, for example, there are no doors on the toilets. There are no doors on the shower room. There are no doors on the manager's room. You've got this big lump of humanity, sports writers walking around, camera crews everywhere, and you're supposed to be doing something social like eating a meal. Let me tell you, that environment is distinctly less than a box social. I can remember leaving the ballpark with my son Bryan one night, I think we were in Cleveland, and he said, "Dad, it's so gross to watch you guys eat after a ball game." A little kid can see how obscene it is, but the adults are so programmed they can't tell the difference anymore—take that for whatever it's worth. The bottom line is that most athletes, in their own environment, are virtually unembarrassable.

Never has the sanctity of the clubhouse been so shattered as the day women sportswriters made their presence felt. It wasn't necessarily threatening, but it was definitely disruptive. You could have made a movie of the social interactions that went on between the female writers as they entered the clubhouse, and the athletes.

The goal of every ballplayer was to be as gross or disarming as humanly possible when a woman reporter was standing around listening or asking questions. But one particular athlete topped them all. This guy was, shall we say, endowed like an uncircumcised horse, and one of his favorite tricks was to put a lit cigarette in the head of his dick and conduct an interview while it was smoking.

Normally, among only the men, this caused a casual remark or a laugh. Nothing unusual, right? Well, one night a female writer came in a little late to the interview, and he was doing his act. She went to ask a question, and at the very moment she opened her mouth, she noticed the cigarette and what it was doing, and she was finished for the night. I mean, she could not get the question out of her mouth. And after she peeled her chin off the floor, she just kind of folded up her notebook and walked out. That's the sort of thing women have had to deal with in the clubhouse.

It's too bad, because most women who have to do their job in the clubhouse do it as professionally as any males, if not more so. There are those who come in to take a look around, who can't get their eyes up above chest-level, but those are the exception by far. They know the rules of the clubhouse, and they play by them. In other words, no matter what they see, they try to do their jobs.

If the clubhouse is secretive, the training rooms are downright vaultlike in their security. There is no press, no media of any kind allowed in the training room. I don't know where that rule came from, but trainers will practically go to war when someone who doesn't belong pops his head in the door, or when someone is goofing around while someone else is getting treatment. It's a place for business, not country-clubbing, as the expression goes. You go in, get your treatment, and get gone.

The trainer in professional baseball has an almost Godlike status. Pitching coaches provide information, managers provide direction, but when you're hurt and you can't play or you're hurt and you want to play and it *hurts* to play, you go to the trainer just like you'd go to Mommy when you were a six-year-old with a skinned knee.

The trainer has an enormous impact on the clubhouse, as he protects his domain the same way a priest protects his parish. He decides who can enter his training room, who can play, who should rest. He also allows athletes to hide out in the training room when they're trying to avoid the media. When a player wants to keep away from writers and/or television and radio people, he will just head into the training room and hang out there until deadlines have to be met and tapings have to be sent in and the media have to leave.

Trainers are the guys who athletes call at 3:30 in the morning when they get an attack of food poisoning and they can't get away from the toilet, or when they've had a little bit too much to drink and they're seeing God, or when they think they have galloping dandruff (crabs) or some semblance of a social disease, or whatever the reason. Anything and everything is taken care of by the trainer.

In the early days before baseball cracked down on drugs, trainers were the guys you went to to get your "help" for the day. They controlled the "cookie jar," as we called it; they held onto it, watched it, traveled with it, packed it, and presided over its contents. This was their role, just as it used to be the role of the clubhouse attendants to play messenger when you wanted to meet a lady you had seen in the stands; the clubhouse guy could deliver a note for you. That was part of the job.

If the clubhouse man acts as wife and mother, providing those tangible things like clothing and food, then the emotional support in this little baseball family comes from the trainer. Everybody in the baseball existence is part of the family, and everybody has a role to play, and trainers do their part by providing the physical and psychological nurturing.

Add to this the traveling secretary, the fellow who, among other things, tells you when to deliver your bags to the ballpark for a road trip; once you deliver them, you don't touch them again for the duration of the trip. They show up in your room on the road, and when you're ready to move on to another city, there are your bags, waiting for you in your new hotel room.

You need tickets? Call the traveling secretary. Need a tee time? He can do it. It's like having your own personal concierge.

When you consider all of these loyal "family" members, is it any wonder ballplayers have trouble adjusting to the *real* world once they're out of baseball? Is it any wonder that they can't make an airline reservation or balance a checkbook? Why should they? In the baseball environment, they don't have to—someone else does it for them.

And while all of this would be completely unacceptable in the real world, it's status quo among baseball ranks. This is the way it's always been done, and this is the way we want it done, says the invisible force, tradition. Tamper with the rules and rituals, and you tamper with the spirit of the game itself.

7
Drugs

Have you heard the good word? Baseball's powers-that-be have—are you ready?— declared the National Pastime on its way to being drug-free! Will wonders never cease? Funny, it seems to me that we're reading about just as many players in drug or alcohol rehabilitation as we were five years ago.

What those powers-that-be *mean* is that teams are making a better show of good PR, as if to say, "All right already, we're concerned, we're concerned. Okay? Now get off our backs!"

Here's where baseball's hypocrisy screams out loud and clear. When a player is hitting .204 and he spends most of his time on the bench, he's completely expendable when his drug problem is discovered by the team. If they trade him or release him, who's going to question the move? The fans and the media will just assume he's being sent away for being a lousy ballplayer. The team won't have to deal with negative publicity, nor will it have to support him in a rehabilitation program. It can quietly and effectively wash its hands of the player. He can become someone else's problem.

Now consider the same situation, but substitute a front-line player—a superstar. He's hitting .320, he's going to have 125 RBIs for the season. If you yank him out of the lineup the fans might just kill the manager, and if you trade him they'll burn down the ballpark. Of course, if you announce his problem and get him some help, you probably won't win as many games, team morale will be shattered, and the media will have a party at your expense. What to do?

The sad but true reality about the competitive world of baseball is when you're performing, you can exhibit aberrant behavior and get away with it. Management is going to ignore your maladaptive habit—it's so much easier to look the other way—as long as you're striking out hitters or batting .300. The team keeps winning, morale stays high, and, after all, if the problem is still there *after* the season, we can deal with it then. No need to rock the boat now.

Isn't it remarkable how many players undergo drug or alcohol rehabilitation as soon as the season ends? Odd coincidence, don't you think? Teams may tell you they had *no idea* that there was a player with a drug problem, but as soon as October rolls around, there's this shocking revelation: "Heaven forbid, drugs in our midst!" I have a hard time believing that from March to October, this player was drugging or drinking, and *nobody* had a clue. It isn't possible. Ballplayers spend too much time together, and management spends too much time with the players, for no one to spot an abuser. But it's easier to turn away than blow the whistle. Then when the season is over, and athletes retreat to their various corners of the earth, suddenly ball clubs are "reaching out" to help their players with their newly discovered problems. Nice gesture, but a bit too late.

Of course, all of this applies only to those players who do have problems, and there's no doubt that the number of players with problems has been widely exaggerated. Baseball is basically a society, and like society in general, there is only a percentage of people with substance-abuse problems. Despite what you may hear or read, drug abuse is not a required behavior in major league baseball, nor is alcoholism. Unfortunately, we hear so much about it because players with problems always make the headlines. And if you believed everything you read, you'd begin to get the impression that players are practically racing to the park every day to sit around the clubhouse and smoke a doob or do a line. Oooh, maybe they all sit in a big circle and . . . forget it, folks, that ain't the way it happens.

And yet there are a significant number of players with drug or alcohol problems, and the obvious question is why. From an outsider's perspective, it seems that if someone is so highly paid to keep his body in top condition, how hard can it be to stay away from drugs? And the obvious cynical answer is usually, "Hey, you give these idiots all that money and they can't wait to piss it all away on alcohol or drugs." A charming theory, but not altogether true. A better analysis might be this: give a professional athlete all that money, and his whole lifestyle changes. Suddenly he has "friends" who can't wait to show him that fast-lane life he's been striving for—the hottest parties, the wildest women, the purest drugs. It's as if it's built into his perceived image of what "success" is all about. Now he has the flash and cash to impress all sorts of people, and just like every other professional athlete, he knows he's invincible—a real Superman. So a little coke isn't going to hurt, right? Just a little, and it'll be out of my system by game time, okay? Hey, you see guys do this stuff all the time and they're just fine, so what's the big deal? And anyway, who's going to know? I got enough pressures to deal with out there, I deserve a little relaxation, and if this takes my mind off the game for a few hours, that's my business.

Fine, but when he starts missing wake-up calls and buses and, eventually, fastballs, it becomes team business, and it becomes the team's decision whether to get this kid immediate help, or, if the team can't seem to spare him, sweat it out and hope the press doesn't catch on.

Baseball's drug situation has become so complex that you can even distinguish between acceptable and unacceptable drugs. The unacceptable variety includes the obvious—cocaine, crack, marijuana, and so forth. The acceptable stuff? The greenies, the diet pills, the amphetamines. They've been a part of the game for decades, as common as chewing tobacco and gum.

There are fewer players popping greenies in today's game than there were when I first signed. Back then, it seemed like in the game of professional baseball, alcohol and amphetamines were the accepted substances to abuse.

I remember one player, a pitcher, who was greened up on a regular basis. He was always in the cookie jar, so to speak, and had achieved some measure of success.

Then there was the first big clean-up, after the 1971 season. I think everyone was talking about getting caught, and management was all intent on not having any drugs in the clubhouse or anywhere near, and players were so afraid of being nailed that they were trying to go clean. Baseball was being heralded as "drug-free" going into the following season.

And this particular player, without his greenies, got off to a horrible start. He couldn't win a game to save his life. About six weeks into the season he's sitting at 1-and-5 with an ERA of . . . well, if he dialed it, he got Bangkok. One day the manager calls him into his office and says, "Hey, are you still taking those amphetamines? Are you still taking greenies?"

And the pitcher says, "No, Goddamn, no, Skip. I gave that shit up just like they told us to."

The manager looks him in the face and hollers, "Well, you better start taking that shit again, or you're going to be out of a job!"

There are marginal athletes, above-average athletes, and Hall of Famers who can't perform, who can't go out and compete, without being on some form of an upper, some form of a greenie. I don't know if the effect is more physical or psychological, but in baseball, it's as commonplace as putting on your shoes. Many players describe it as being "as if the lights were suddenly turned on. It's like you flip a switch and you're ready to go." If they have a lousy game anyway, the philosophy is, "I didn't get beat, I just got out-greened." And all the information and education and communication in the world isn't going to make sense to this guy, because when he is succeeding, he feels like he succeeds with more consistency when he is taking greenies. The fact that greenies are considered illegal is basically meaningless to players who have easy access through various networks, and the legal alternative, caffeine, is considered too ridiculously impractical to even think about. Says one player, "What am I supposed to do, spend all day slugging down coffee, and then spend the whole game in the john?"

Back in the fifties, the only substances being abused were alcohol and amphetamines. No one had heard of "pot" yet—and cocaine? What the heck is that? It wouldn't have mattered anyway, because no ballplayer made enough money then to afford it.

Then came the Vietnam era, the hippies and the flower children, and basically, the youngsters of that era were into anything that could be ingested. If you couldn't snort it, you smoked it; if you couldn't smoke it, you ate it; if you couldn't eat it, you put it in the blender and sprinkled it on your brownies.

That was the attitude that ballplayers of my age

group were exposed to. I can remember hearing someone say you can get off on banana peels. We smoked banana peels. You can smoke dirty gym socks. We tried dirty gym socks. You would go to parties and people would say, "Here, take this," and you had no idea what you were taking, but you took it because it was the thing to do. Nobody knew. The information and the communication about the information were nonexistent. And managers and coaches didn't have a clue, because all of this was so new.

In the seventies, the name of the game was defying the system. People were beginning to realize that this stuff was *bad*, and being caught could be worse. So hard-core, nonintelligent use of drugs gave way to the notion of, "We're going to have to beat the system if we don't want to get in trouble." The trend shifted toward sophistication: do your drug, be it alcohol, be it marijuana, be it Quaaludes, whatever, but get smart about learning how not to get caught. Ball clubs were bringing in "experts" to lecture on the dangers of doing drugs, and it was pretty standard for at least a half-dozen players to come to one of these meetings wasted, and for one other guy to show up with baby powder all over his nose, sneezing and reducing the entire team into hysterical laughter. Meeting's over, hope you learned something.

With the eighties came a much better information system and a more advanced way of communicating the message, "Just say no." Now you had players—big-name players—serving suspensions, going to rehab programs, going to jail. And still, there is little fear motivating players to stay away from drugs. For example, in professional basketball, repeat offenders know they will be banned from their sport—their livelihood—if they continue to use drugs. In baseball, users know that baseball's creed is "protect your own" and that like many users before them, they can coast through unnoticed, unreported, unexposed. If by chance they are forced to enter a rehab program, they know that like many before them, they'll be welcomed back into the fold with open arms, no repercussions. What if there's a random test or two—just learn how to mask it.

And let's face it: you can't take someone with a serious abuse problem, put him into a nifty little four-week program, and expect him to come out cured for life. You can't put him back into the same environment he was in before—same friends, same lifestyle—and expect a total change. But when you consider the thought processes of the ballplayer, you realize his attitude is, "I can do this easily because I do everything easily." He stays in rehab the requisite four weeks, and as the vast public heralds his triumphant return, he plunges back into the same behaviors that helped screw him up in the first place. Four weeks of "training" cannot arm him for combat with old habits.

Most ball clubs don't take the rehab process far enough, either. Their priority is to get the player back to the team, where he can help the ball club. It's a business decision. A club is paying a player so much to perform, and his personal life is his business. The team's business is baseball, so as long as the player is performing, it's going to do everything possible to *keep* him performing. It's a short-term remedy to a very long-term problem: the team manages to squeeze another year or two out of the player before he self-destructs—maybe it can even win a pennant with him. All the while the player is trapped in this Catch-22: if he asks for help the team looks bad for not helping sooner (plus he suffers the public humiliation), and if he doesn't ask for help he just gets sicker. No way out.

This scenario even becomes stranger when you consider fan reaction to ballplayers with abuse problems. People like Dwight Gooden or Keith Hernandez survive their drug habits and return to the field to the roar of cheers and ovations, because they are bona fide stars: without them in the lineup, people can only envision playoff dreams going down the toilet. But a more ordinary player endures a nightmare's worth of boos and jeers; after all, he should be lucky just to be in the majors, right? Whadda bum, screwing up his life like that. He finds out the hard way that no one cares what kind of person you are, only what sort of player you are. *That's* your identity.

Now, lest I give you the impression I'm just mouthing off and cursing baseball for the weaknesses of a handful of players, let me remind you that, as I said earlier in this book, there's very little I've talked about here that I haven't actually experienced, tried, done, snorted, abused, used, whatever. I've been there. Certainly not with the intensity of someone like a Steve Howe or Alan Wiggins or LaMarr Hoyt, but enough that I remember one night after a game when I was back in my hotel room getting ready to do a certain substance, and I accidentally dropped it. I went nuts, like a starving man who had just watched his last meal disappear. At that moment of temporary insanity I just happened to be standing in front of a mirror, and caught the reflection of the crazed look on my face. I saw that the person in the mirror was not who I wanted to be.

I literally scared myself into deciding to go straight. At that moment, I put on my clothes and went down the hall where some of my buddies were partying and said, "Look, I love you guys, but you can color my ass gone. I'm out of this. I've got to move into other things."

For about a year after I decided to clean up my act, I had lost my identity as a player: the straight players still didn't want to deal with me because they thought I was doing drugs, and the druggies didn't want to have anything to do with me (nor I them) because I had walked away from the "scene." It wasn't as if everyone suddenly ignored me, or that I stopped being competitive on the field; I just suddenly didn't have a peer group to relate to, to fit in with. And as we know, in the baseball life, you are judged by the group you run with. So for many ex-users, and certainly for me, the whole structure of the baseball society makes it somewhat less than easy to give up your role as a user.

All of which leads us, of course, to the subject of drug testing. Is it a violation of rights or a way to save lives? Does a player's right to privacy outweigh another player's right to a clean, drug-free life? Players who don't do drugs are objecting on the privacy issue, and those who do drugs are objecting to save their skins. But there's more to it than that. The obvious question always arises: if you're not involved with drugs, then why not just take the test? Ah, it comes back to the subject we discussed earlier: you protect your own. Sure, says a player, I'm clean, but what if our star hitter isn't? Forget it, he says, you're not getting any of us.

The issue will have to be settled eventually, and the ethical questions are too enormous to answer here. I do know that players fear drug testing for many reasons other than fear of getting caught: they fear the margin for error, they fear the possibility of tampering. And no one has yet been able to present the players with a viable plan for testing.

The answer? I don't have it, but I'm sure that as soon as someone finds a way to rid society of drugs, say, in the next thousand years or so, baseball will be rid of drugs as well. Until then, as long as players have that "jock's itch" to scratch, there will be players turning to drugs for relief. And unless management stops protecting players in trouble, we'll keep on reading and hearing about one more player who "suddenly" turns up in rehab.

8
Money

H ow can you fine a player for breaking curfew when he probably owns half the hotel?" So goes the saying about baseball's
new moneyed breed, for whom the game has most
definitely become a business. It's hard to imagine
that when Abner Doubleday invented baseball, he
intended for independent arbitrators to determine
how much a player should be paid for a specific
performance, or that someone would create an
evaluation system for rating exactly how much a
player is worth, or that there would someday be
players who earned as much money in one at-bat
as some people do in a year. But that is indeed how
it is done today, and there are some very wealthy
athletes as a result.

The relationship between ballplayers and their
money is best summed up by equating it to the
relationship between teenagers and their money.

Consider a teenager with a new job and a sudden pocketful of cash. He can't wait to get out and show off to his friends, and he's buying everything in sight: a great car, a stereo, cool clothes, maybe something for his girlfriend.

The terminally adolescent athlete has the same priorities. He knows just what to do with his money: spend it. Remember, few players simply show up in the big leagues one day with their pockets bulging with cash; most come up the hard way, after years of lousy pay and little pocket change. When they finally hit paydirt, they can't spend it fast enough.

Let's take a look at the financial birthing of an average ballplayer. At the age of eighteen, he is a prospect right out of high school, probably from a middle-class or lower-middle-class community. Whatever he gets paid, it's going to look like a lot, especially if he gets one of those signing bonuses with all the zeroes attached.

I remember getting my first taste of the real world when, still in the minor leagues, with a wife who was seven months pregnant, she and I opened a checking account. Wow! Our own checking account—with a credit line—heady stuff. Before long we had our own bounced checks, and when we got our own credit cards, we loaded them up to our very own limit. Isn't money great?

But, hey, I still had the second half of my signing bonus coming, about $23,000, so why worry? Money, money everywhere. I was recuperating from knee surgery, and while we were both dealing with bouncing checks and credit cards and the arguments that go with all of the above, and somehow, we sort of . . . well, I guess there is no other way of saying it: we blew the second half of my bonus, all $23,000 in about three and a half months.

To this day I really can't tell you *how* we spent it or *why* we spent it. We just did, because when you're young and suddenly you have that much money, you just *have* to spend it. So I bought a Porsche with bigger wheels and a bigger stereo than anyone else ever saw on the block. And we bought clothes for the wife, who was feeling depressed because she was very pregnant with our first child and she was getting big, so we did a lot of things to keep her ego going. It was only chips, not like losing friends, and anyway, we had money to burn.

Or so we thought. I mean, we never really stopped to consider that this money was not falling off of trees, that it had a source and the source was going to eventually dry up. It just never occurred to us. And it is this very frame of mind that every ballplayer carries with him through his career, as he earns more and more, and spends more and more, never looking ahead or looking back. Spend what you have; there will surely be more.

No matter what stage of his career a player may be in, he cannot distinguish between great big money and little bitty money. Most players worry more about how much they have to tip the waiter at dinner or what they're going to pay a cabbie than they do about their million-dollar salaries; money that big is just numbers on paper.

I knew a guy who was making over a million dollars a year, but he'd fight like hell when it came to tipping a cab driver, or when he was sure a cabbie was taking advantage of him by taking the wrong route. No one ever wanted to share a ride with him because of the inevitable argument he was going to have with the driver, accusing him of trying to charge him too much, and hollering, "Whaddaya mean, $4.50? I took a cab here yesterday for $4.30. What kinda crap is this?" It was embarrassing, not only to watch the poor driver trembling at the steering wheel, but to know that this player was making more per season than any cab driver would ever see in a lifetime.

It's as if the "big" money isn't even real. Oh, it looks good on a check, and all those zeroes and commas sure take up a lot of space, but reality goes as far as what is in a player's pocket—what he can spend right now. I remember dropping by the room of a very successful player—way into the six figure salary category—and there on the dresser were at least six checks, some in envelopes, some not, just lying there. And these were not $1.98 refund checks from cereal box tops. These were checks for $10,000 and $15,000, and I'm perspiring just being close to so much money.

"Are you nuts?" I asked. "Do you have any idea how stupid this is, leaving all this money lying around? Do you know how much money this is?"

He was totally unfazed. "Yeah, yeah, I know." He waved me off. "I'll take care of it. Christ, you're just like my agent, always on my case about money."

And then he added the ultimate ballplayer's

credo: "Anyway, it's just a bunch of checks. It's not like I'm leaving real money around. If you lose a check, you can always get another." Which is, of course, true for a star athlete. No problem, Mr. Pitcher, we'll be happy to take care of that for you today.

When it comes to the marriage between ballplayers and money, the motto is "The rich get richer ... and richer and richer." The bigger your salary, the more people want you to dine in their restaurants, shop in their stores, drive their cars—and it's all on the house. Of course, this makes absolutely no sense, since those big-money players are precisely the people who can afford to *buy* those things without a second thought. The baseball pyramid is totally upside down when it comes to good deals and freebies. Minor leaguers, who barely make enough to eat at McDonald's three times a day, need all the help they can get, while the big leaguers have twenty-eight pairs of shoes and seventeen different gloves, and they get paid for the privilege of having them. Fly into any city and head straight to the nearest Polo outlet, where any self-respecting player can buy clothes at twenty cents on the dollar. And don't forget to ask about those free passes to various nightclubs and Broadway shows. When you're a ballplayer and you play your cards right, you may never again have to pay for anything yourself.

But there has to be a catch, and it is this: once those playing days are over, you pay. You pay for everything. Suddenly, restaurants aren't so quick to pick up the check; the guy who gives you Laker tickets hasn't been returning your calls. I know a player—a major star for many years—who was forced to retire mid-season because of a sudden injury. The plaster was barely dry on his cast when his "friends" at the auto dealership wanted their Mercedes back. Ah, welcome back to the real world.

Understandably, ex-players tend to get fairly pissed off when last year they could get a bank loan over the phone, and now that they're out of the game they have to document their life history and sign in blood just to get in the door. But the fact that this happens to virtually every player who has retired from the game is further proof that few players can accept the fact that their baseball existence is completely transient and temporary. No one wants to admit that the big dollars and big salaries are a strikeout away from disappearing.

Why should they? There's money everywhere. To give this some perspective, consider the numbers. The *average* major league salary is $412,500, not including road trip money (for meals, taxis, whatever), which is $47 per day—what you don't spend you keep. Mike Schmidt once said that he could live off his meal money and never touch his salary, and some old-timer managers and coaches insist that today's meal money is bigger than their salaries when they played years ago.

Then there are the appearances fees (for example, in 1987 Orel Hershiser was barely getting $1,500 an appearance; today post-World Series engagements are bringing in no less than $10,000 a pop). There are licensing revenues that players share from the sale of all those "official" baseball goodies with the team emblems and from the car deals, shoe deals, glove deals, bat deals, not to mention commercials (and some of them are so bad they *shouldn't* be mentioned). And remember, all of this money is going directly into the players' pockets independent of paychecks.

The new gig is the baseball card shows, where players get paid thousands of dollars to show up, *plus* a percentage of the sale price of every card they autograph. So basically, you're getting paid for your ability to sign your own name.

So what does a player do with all his newfound wealth? Mostly, he mismanages it, if he manages it at all. If you take the top one hundred businessmen in the nation and compare their salaries to those of baseball's top one hundred money-makers, the result will make it appear that ballplayers are cleaning up. But consider: businessmen earn their dollars over a lifetime, and they've made their money by understanding money. Ballplayers make their money by playing with a ball, and they do it all in an average of four to five years. Within those few years, they have the opportunity to make either some very smart decisions or some very dumb ones, and the fact that an enormous percentage of ex-players have gone bankrupt after their playing days ended should tell you exactly how those decisions went. The bottom line is that professional athletes are, generally, lousy money managers. Why? Because it takes common sense and maturity to make smart money decisions (especially when the money in question adds up to seven figures), and most players have a distinct lack of either.

From a fan's perspective, it must seem so strange: all these players making all this money, and somehow managing to blow it all within a year of their retirement. You can't blame the average fan for shaking his head at the newspaper, smirking, "Those fools . . . they get all that money and they either blow it up their noses or piss it away on cars and jewelry. Man, what I could do with that kind of money. Ballplayers must be damn stupid." Maybe, but more likely they're just unprepared to deal with such fast and furious wealth.

As embarrassing as it is for a player to lose huge amounts of money (or worse, go bankrupt), it's twice as embarrassing to know that millions of fans are going to read about your troubles in the newspaper and snicker about the situation. You can spend years building up your image and becoming a role model and hero, but as soon as you run into financial problems, you get knocked off the pedestal pretty darn fast. You've just become one of the common folk: the average Joe might not be able to hit a fastball, but he knows he can balance a checkbook.

Big dollars have not only warped the fan's view of players, they have also affected his view of the game itself. "Sure," the fan says. "A million-six for this free agent, and he still can't get the ball over the plate." Sound familiar? It's the cry of the disgruntled observer, who can't figure out why a guy who's hitting .237 is making more money in a single day than he makes in a month. As a result, fans have begun to view the game in terms of "pay versus performance"; as if it's more justifiable for a low-paid player to strike out than a high-paid player. Surely there's some truth in that theory— the more you're paid, the more you're expected to produce—but when expectations are based exclusively on salary, something's wrong.

These days it's fashionable for people both in and out of baseball to bemoan the notion that "the game has become a business," as if it was ever anything else. The accusations are varied: "Agents are ruining the game." "No player deserves that much money." "That owner is so cheap—he should pay the player what he's worth." I'm sure that as the numbers have grown larger, the crying has grown louder, but I don't think the business side of the game has ever really changed. True, twenty years ago agents weren't nearly as common as they are today, and the million-dollar player was yet a twinkle in some outfielder's eye, but the theory that baseball has been infested with buttoned-down millionaires who read *The Wall Street Journal* in the dugout is grossly exaggerated. They do exist, but they're few and far between.

The truth is that the vast majority of professional athletes play the game simply because *they love the game.* They also love the money, and they're more than willing to accept today's wildly inflated salaries. But does that mean they care any less about the game than the men who played before them, when some of the greatest stars who *ever* played the game made less than $20,000 a year? Does Don Mattingly care less about being a

baseball player than Ted Williams did, just because he makes a zillion times more money? Of
course not.

It's just that today there's so much more money
being generated, and if the players *didn't* look for a
share of it, they'd be crazy. Today you have television revenues, advertising revenues, and many of
the things we mentioned before, like licensing income and endorsements. And you have teams
owned by corporations like the Tribune Co. (Chicago) or multi-millionaires like George Stein-
brenner and Peter O'Malley who can afford to pay
the high salaries. But it sure doesn't indicate that
players are only in the game for the money.

Look at it this way: If you were told that your
career was going to be great but it was only going
to last for five years, wouldn't you try to amass all
the wealth you could while you still had a job?
That's all the athlete is trying to do. He knows that
whatever he does after his sports career, it sure
isn't going to pay anything close to what he was
making as a player. So on the advice of his agent,
he arbitrates, declares free agency, and he holds
out for the best possible contract, shows up at all
sorts of appearances, and collects as much of the
wealth as he can, before it's all over. Because it's
always over much too soon.

9
Getting Out

You never think it's going to happen, but one day, there you are at the end of the line. Since childhood, you have been a hero, a star. And now, at an age when other men your age are just blossoming into their careers, yours is done. You're all through.

You have been trained for little else, and even if you had been trained for something else, it wouldn't matter, because you really don't want to *do* anything else. You really haven't thought about a career after the game, after baseball, except maybe for those thoughts you had about a broadcasting or coaching career, but no one's called to offer you a job.

You go from a big salary to none at all, and unless you have been fortunate enough to have an agent who knew how to provide you with deferred income, you're not sure how long the money in the bank will last.

Your whole calendar is different. You get the itch again in the first week of February, but you've got no place to go. You're not going to spring training. The season is here, and it's starting without you. You're watching games on TV instead of watching from the mound.

And suddenly, you realize that what Jim Bouton said about the game of baseball is true: you spend years and years gripping a baseball, and in the end you realize that all along it's been gripping you, and gripping you good. Whether you're in or out of uniform, it's going to do that for the rest of your life.

Now you have to ask yourself questions you never thought you'd have to worry about: How is this retirement, or this release, this pink slip, going to affect your marriage? What about your relationship with your kids? What about your sense of financial security? What about your self-image, your self-esteem?

Has there ever been a ballplayer who made a graceful exit from the game? How can this game draw its participants, its constituents, so close, and then turn its back when the party is over?

There is a saying that old athletes never die, they just lose their athletic supporters. It sounds funny, but that's just the way it is. Consider the Old-Timers Games. I have been fortunate to play in a couple of them, and I've watched a few others being played. The only way to describe the experience is as a time warp. To the old-timers, it's as if nothing has ever changed.

Some of these men are Hall of Famers, some of

them are hangers-on; some of them are healthy, some of them are not so healthy; some of them are infirm, and some are in pretty good shape; the whole spectrum of human strengths and frailties is visible in these old-timers.

They come to feel old feelings, to look down the bench and see themselves sitting with the Joe Di-Maggios and the Willie Mayses and the Henry Aarons and the Frank Robinsons and the Bob Gibsons, you name 'em. These are guys of my generation, older than my generation, and *way* older than my generation. But the thrill is still the same. The interaction, the camaraderie, the clubhouse banter, the dugout chatter, the spark, the light in their eyes is the same in these games as it was when they were players. And it's the same spark and light that you see in the eyes of the youngsters who play ball for a living today. It gives you goose bumps to look at it. It also makes you realize that the athlete is an athlete is an athlete, and will always be.

Joe DiMaggio. I have been in three Old-Timers Games with him. He takes his bows. He sits on the bench. He rides around and waves at the fans. And when he sits on the bench, he's deferred to just like he was when he was a player, just as someone like Don Mattingly is deferred to in today's game.

The Lew Burdettes and the Warren Spahns have the same mannerisms they used to; their bodies don't react to the mannerisms as they did when they were playing, but the competitive spark, the pride they take in their profession, and the love they have for the game is just as intense. Some of these coots haven't been in a competitive baseball game for thirty years, yet you see the same reactions, the same approaches, the same subtleties, the same nonverbal communication that you see in contemporary athletes who are performing in today's game.

So read my lips, Mom. You may get them out of the game, but you never get them *from* the game.

Let's talk about the anatomy of a "nonvoluntary" retirement, also known as a career-threatening release. Early in your career, as you are trying to get to the big leagues, you'll do anything to *earn* a job. Once you establish yourself as a major leaguer and things are going well and you know you've got a job, you're always trying to determine what you have to do to *keep* the job.

Then, as you get older, you start feeling the ground swell from underneath, as the talent from below starts to make its presence felt. And even if you have a guaranteed contract, you start to realize that as you get a little older, it's not as easy to get yourself ready to do what you have done easily and taken for granted in the past.

It's in this phase of your life that you look for a role on the ball club that will make the best use of what you can do and perhaps call less attention to what you can't do.

But you begin to decline—yes, even you—and before long comes the inevitable pink slip. You don't see it as the result of not doing the job; you see it as the result of not getting the opportunity to *do* your job.

I have never heard an athlete, a released athlete or a retired athlete or a traded athlete, who has not expressed the thought, "Just give me the opportunity, and I will do exactly what I did five years ago." In their own minds, this positive denial allows them the comfort of believing that it wasn't lack of talent, it was lack of opportunity. It's the same thought process that gets them to the big leagues in the first place.

Talent lets you perform in the big leagues, and experience keeps you around when your talent declines. And it's at the point, when your talent no longer supports the experience that you have (in other words, when the hardware can no longer do what the software is telling it to), that you're on thin ice; you're going to be released. You may still have flashes of greatness, and you might get lucky now and then, but the reality is that when the talent no longer supports the experience, the dance is almost over.

There are those sentimental favorites, the superstars, who can hang around a year or two longer than they should simply because of who they have been—a Reggie Jackson, a Steve Garvey, a Pete Rose. You hear fans screaming that "those old guys" just take up space on the roster, that they command big salaries, that they should move over to make way for the new regime. But these players contribute in ways other than what you may see on the field. They offer veteran experience, and that can't be manufactured; you either have it or you don't. They've earned the right to decide when *they* want to leave the game. Of course, the organization may nudge them along a bit, but it will be discreet; future Hall of Famers don't get released, they just gracefully retire. Or so it seems. Behind the scenes they're shaking their heads and saying, "I can't believe they're starting that kid in my position." But for the public eye, they call a press conference and announce their decision to retire.

Unfortunately, most players don't have that luxury. Like most athletes, I fought for every job I ever had. I earned those jobs. I managed to hang onto them, but when the decline begins, there's nothing you can do. For me, the decline began in Boston. I was playing for the Red Sox and basically stinking up the place. It was the beginning of the end, although I didn't know it at the time. No athlete ever does. I just figured I was having a rough season, either because I'd been injured or because I was just in a little slump, or any one of a million excuses.

From there I went to Seattle. Okay, I was an experienced pitcher on an expansion ball club, and I did a fairly good job for a couple of seasons, putting up some adequate numbers. But still, my skills weren't what they once had been, even though my experience and my know-how and my savvy enabled me to perform. My ability was declining, and I got released. This was a team with a youth movement, and they took a liking to two "youngsters," Rick Honeycutt and Shane Rawley, releasing Jim Colborn and me. Of course, Jim and I were incensed because we had both had pretty good springs, but we'd both spent enough years in the game to know what to expect. I knew subconsciously that this was going to be my last spring training no matter how well I performed.

When the decision has been made by the organization, consciously or unconsciously, nothing is going to change its mind. No matter how good you do or how bad you do, when you're history, you're history. It's like the umpires; they make a decision and find a reason to back it up.

Anyway, I had a great spring and so did Jim Colborn, but we ended up getting released on the last day of spring training.

Getting released is one of the strangest feelings there is in baseball. You go to the ballpark as usual and everything is great. People talk to you, make eye contact. You jibber and jabber and you do your normal game-day things. And you get your uniform on and suddenly, there it is: the tap on the shoulder. The killer is that the tap comes just before you're ready to go out on the field to get yourself loose for the day, and you're asking God, "Can't I just have today?"

But it's a matter of economy. They don't want to pay you for the extra day, blah blah blah. When you get tapped on the shoulder, it's time to go.

You go into the office, you listen to the bullshit reasons why you're being released, reasons that are absolutely idiotic to you, but they sure seem to make sense to management. It doesn't really matter anyway, because you're too twisted up inside to hear what they're saying.

Then you walk back into the clubhouse, and suddenly nobody will look at you. It's like you now have leprosy or the plague or whatever. You no longer exist.

At the time, I really took it personally. I said,

"Hey, look at me. I'm still the same person I was twenty minutes ago. I just don't have a fucking uniform on my back anymore. You guys don't like me anymore just because I got released?"

And there's some nervous laughter, and they all get the hell out of there fast because they're a little embarrassed for you. They can't look at you or don't want to look at you because it reminds them of their own frailties and their insecurities, and they realize that what just happened to you is eventually going to happen to them. No one likes to be reminded of reality.

I packed up my stuff, paid my clubhouse dues, made a few jokes, and jumped in the car to head for home. Completely numb, I must have done about ninety miles an hour between Phoenix and home in San Diego, playing games with myself all the way, "All right. No biggie. I will find a job somewhere. I don't care where it is. I will find a job."

Got home, got a little support from family and kids: "Hey, Dad, nice to have you home." Started making phone calls, trying to find a job. No good; there just were none available.

But you do anything to stay in the game, right? So I ended up going down to Latin America and playing in this Inter-American League, which was a new concept in professional baseball. Instead of winter ball, this was summertime baseball in Latin America, which was a new experience.

I was paid top dollar to go down to Caracas, Venezuela, and the money was only my rationalization for going. The real reason was that it was baseball. I was in a uniform. But there I was, full of resentment, full of frustration, putting up some pretty good numbers but hating every minute of it. Seven-hour customs checks going into the Dominican Republic. Flight schedules all screwed up. Starting times with two-and-a-half-hour delays. We were playing a game in Panama when the Sandinistas blew through there on their way to Nicaragua. Exciting stuff.

Finally the league folded just before the Fourth of July, and I showed up at home in time for the holiday completely burned out on baseball.

I was home about five or six days when I got a call from the San Diego Padres offering me a job pitching for their Hawaii franchise, Triple-A ball for embarrassing money, but it was a job in baseball, right? Believe it or not, I passed it by.

Why? My wife pretty much made up my mind for me. She said, "Okay, go ahead, but I'm going to divorce you if you do." She couldn't stand the thought of me going through life grovelling and willing to take any job in baseball just so I could stay in a jockstrap. End of thought process on whether to play minor league baseball.

How did I adjust to a nonbaseball life? Well, I adjusted real well. I grew a beard, went to the beach at ten o'clock every morning, and didn't come home until dark. For about three months.

And then, as wives and children will do, they kind of brought me out of the fog toward the end of what amounted to the regular major league season. My wife said, "Don't you think it's time to get a grip on things here, Thomas?" And I said, "Well, what do you mean, get a grip on things?" She said, "Well, the money is running a little short, and it's time for us to think about other things."

So I got real smart and I bought a retailing business, thinking I was going to become an entrepreneur in the casual wear/sporting goods business. It took me only three and a half years to go bankrupt, but I did.

But while I was in the process of losing over a million dollars, I joined the community, still posturing as a ballplayer, playing local citizen and contributing businessman, good husband and good father, and all that bullshit, but I was miserable, literally miserable every moment of my existence. Nothing seemed to scratch the itch.

Finally a friend of mine, Bob Cluck, who was a player development guy for the Houston Astros, called. He said, "How would you like to be a pitching coach for the Houston Astros?"

I said, "Yeah, where? Big leagues, Triple-A? Tell me all about it."

"No," he said, "we got a job for you in the rookie league come June."

I said, "Let me think about it."

I would have turned the job down, except when spring training rolled around, I got that old familiar call of the wild and said, "Okay, I'm willing to consider it. I've got my stores and I'm doing this and I'm doing that, but I'm willing to consider it."

So, they flew me down to Cocoa Beach, Florida, I met Bill Virdon and the gang, and within an hour I said, "Yeah, I miss this. This is me." So, bright person that I was, I said, "I'm going to do both. I'm going to be a minor league pitching coach, *and* I'm going to continue to run my stores."

I won't even try to tell you how screwed up an existence that was. The only time I was happy, the only time I felt right, was when I was on the field, sitting on the bench, or in the bullpen working with pitchers, doing my baseball thing. But I was racing home, clear across the country, two weekends per month, because I had to attend to business. I knew where I wanted to be, but I knew that financially and responsibility wise, I should have been home full-time. But I just couldn't leave baseball. It just didn't feel right. Everything else was faking it. The only place I felt comfortable was in baseball. The only time I was happy was in baseball.

Now other things started entering into the equation. I started feeling guilty about the fact that I would rather be in a baseball uniform than home with my family living a regular existence. But I continued to do both for about three years. I continued to be a minor league pitching coach for Bob Cluck and the Astros until Cluck went over to the Padres. Then I went with him to the Padres minor league teams. I bounced around from Columbus to Reno to Amarillo to Las Vegas.

Then I went belly-up in 1984 and lost everything, I mean everything. We lost about $1,100,000 and equity. I walked away from that part of my life with about $5,500 in cash, an Isuzu Impulse, and a Triple-A job with the San Diego Padres in Las Vegas.

We sold our house, rented a home, and tried to get our lives in order.

About six and a half months after we declared

bankruptcy, two days before Christmas, the house we were leasing burned to the ground. We got out of there with whatever was in the garage. Everything else was destroyed, either by the fire, or the smoke, or the water from the firemen trying to put out the fire.

Not every athlete who gets released from baseball goes through bankruptcy and has his house burn to the ground, but every one of them does have difficulty adjusting. They're not accustomed to fending for themselves, taking responsibility, and making smart personal decisions. Baseball has always been there to do those things for them, and now baseball is gone.

But I survived. I won't say I was lucky; I paid my dues. I paid mentally, emotionally, financially, securitywise, egowise, everything. I was one of the fortunate ones—fortunate that the combination of things didn't destroy my personal and married life. I came out of my postcareer crisis intact, albeit beaten up a little. I went back to school and got my doctorate in psychology so that I could maybe hang out a shingle as a sports psychologist. I became a licensed nutritionist.

Best of all, I was still in the game. I was still satisfying the crazed need I had to be in the comfort zone and still be happy at the job I was working at. Even though the separations were hard, even though the lifestyle stunk, even though the money wasn't even close to what it had been when I was a player, I was still doing the things that made me comfortable in my day-to-day existence.

I resolved in my mind the battle between short-changing my family and my wife at the expense of feeling good about what I was working at, by making up my mind that I was going to improve myself. I was going to be the best at what I did. I would do everything else I possibly could to generate income to get our lifestyle back to where it belonged, to where we were used to being when I was a player.

I did everything. I ran clinics. I taught at San Diego State. I wrote books. I did nutritional workups. I worked at the San Diego School of Baseball. I would dig ditches. I would do anything I could to earn a buck, and I still do to this day, eight years later. I am still putting in eighteen- and twenty-hour days, and have just begun to feel that I'm providing for my wife and children like I should, and that I'm not just stroking my ego by allowing myself to stay in the game of baseball.

But it's worth every minute, because in exchange for all the work, I've been able to stay in baseball. In that sense, I've been luckier than many former players who may not have gone bankrupt and had their houses burn down, but who haven't been allowed to stay in the game, either. And I'm pretty sure that, given a choice between the two, most ex-players would endure everything I did in order to have one more shot at life in baseball.

The truth is: no activity, no job, no pastime can ever be as intensely satisfying, fulfilling, and rewarding as an athlete's involvement in his sport. And you'd have to look far and wide to find an ex-player who wouldn't get back in uniform if he was asked. As one retired player once said, "I've got a great job and make good money, but I'd trade it all to be back in the Texas League on a dirty bus."

In his book *Life on the Run,* ex-basketball star Senator Bill Bradley wrote of what he perceives as a sort of Faustian bargain that all athletes make in exchange for the glory of being a professional athlete:

"In return for fame and fortune, the athletes must live with never again experiencing the intensity or a degree of involvement provided by sports once the sports career is over. During and in, all through both of these stages, the ex-player faces social and economic difficulties. Loss of social recognition is almost immediate. Athletes in the United States are quickly forgotten by once ardent fans and media. Even friends 'seem to disappear' when they can no longer share in the glory."

That sums up the experience of an athlete getting out of the game. But what of the others who have to share the experience, the wives and children and family members who have been local celebrities simply by virtue of their association with a ballplayer? They too have to make the transition, and accept the fact that their bragging rights are going to be significantly diminished once he is out of the game.

Wives, in particular, have a lot of adjusting and coping to deal with. On one hand, a wife realizes what her husband is going through, and wants to be there for him to help him through this personal crisis. But at the same time, she's experiencing a crisis of her own, and there is no one for her to turn to. Unfortunately, many marriages do not survive the transition. There have been some statistics cited recently indicating that the rate of divorce and separation among newly retired athletes is close to 80 percent. I heard one ex-player comment on that figure by smirking, "It'd be even higher, but how many ex-players can afford a divorce?"

Aside from the marital problems, there are also some harsh economic realities to be dealt with. Average salaries are high but average careers are short. Even pensioned athletes don't qualify to start drawing on their pensions until they're forty-five years old. Few athletes can maintain their professional sports lifestyle following retirement. Therefore, most ex-players become virtually overwhelmed as financial pressures compound personal problems. This is the final piece in this abnormal puzzle: it suddenly becomes obvious that they must start living in the "real" world, even though they have no skills to work with. Says one former player: "Looking back, I realize the mental atrophy associated with the game really does affect the way you interpret real life. And it's been real tough for me to make my brain catch up to where it should be, so that I can compete in the real world."

When you talk to former players, you realize that you're hearing the same sentiments repeated over and over, as if they've all lived the same life, the same existence. And, in one respect, they have. Consider the thoughts of these ex-ballplayers:

*   *   *   *

"All of us have self-worth and self-esteem.   Inside you know how you're good. As a matter of fact, in my case, I feel damn good. However, how can you express this outside of baseball? You know what you were, and you know what you should be in the real world. But it just ain't fucking there."

*   *   *   *

"I'm straddling the fence. After three years, I'm still a part-time local truck line supervisor and a part-time coach for the local Jaycee team. Is this fair? I used to strike out Johnny Bench with the bases loaded."

*   *   *   *

"Invariably there will be something that triggers a recall of some baseball situation, and I will look at this particular occurrence through my baseball eyes even though I haven't had a jockstrap on for five years."

*   *   *   *

"I'm trying to make a go of it in the real world, and I hate it when people want to talk about baseball when I'm trying to do a real-world job, sell a product or do my job as a national sales representative. But I will use baseball to get my foot in the door. It's really confusing."

*   *   *   *

"In business situations when someone is getting the better of me, I will go back to my baseball stuff and say, 'The S.O.B. can't hold my jock.' Or 'Put a bat in his hand and I'll get him, I'll show him just how good he is.' And I haven't pitched in thirteen years."

*   *   *   *

And yet, ask any former ballplayer, anyone who has left the game and lived to tell about it, how he'd do it differently, and there isn't one who will tell you he wishes he hadn't played the game. You hear former players say things like, "I used baseball and baseball used me," but you never hear someone *blame* the game for his postbaseball problems.

I don't suppose there will ever again be anything in my life that compares with the thrill I experienced when I was playing baseball, no matter what I do throughout the rest of my life. I enjoy coaching today, but it's sometimes hard to forget that that used to be *me* on that mound. When you're back on the field, hearing your own heart and holding the ball in your hand, it's sometimes hard to remember whether you're fourteen or forty.

Tom House lives in Del Mar, California, with his wife, Karren, and their three children, Brittany, Brooke, and Bryan. He is the pitching coach for the Texas Rangers and a former major-league pitcher for the Atlanta Braves, Boston Red Sox, and Seattle Mariners. He earned his Ph.D. in psychology with a dissertation on the terminal adolescence syndrome among professional athletes. Tom has also done coaching and scouting for the Houston Astros and the San Diego Padres, and is the author of *Contemporary Guide to Pitching*, *The Winning Pitcher*, and *The Diamond Appraised*.